HOW A POEM MOVES

A Field Guide for Readers of Poetry

ADAM SOL

Published by ECW Press
665 Gerrard Street East
Toronto, Ontario, Canada, M4M 1Y2
416-694-3348 / info@ecwpress.com

Editor for the press: Michael Holmes/
a misFit Book

 Cover design: Brienne Lim
Author photo: © Mark Raynes Roberts

LIBRARY AND ARCHIVES CANADA
CATALOGUING IN PUBLICATION

Sol, Adam, 1969-, author
    How a poem moves : a field guide for
readers of poetry / Adam Sol.

Issued in print and electronic formats.
ISBN 978-1-77041-456-3 (softcover)
ISBN 978-1-77305-318-9 (PDF)
ISBN 978-1-77305-317-2 (ePub)

1. Poetry—Appreciation. 2. Poetry—
Explication—Handbooks, manuals, etc.
I. Title.

PN1042.S66 2019   808.1
C2018-905349-6   C2018-905350-X

The publication of *How a Poem Moves* has been generously supported by the Canada Council
for the Arts which last year invested $153 million to bring the arts to Canadians throughout the
country and is funded in part by the Government of Canada. *Nous remercions le Conseil des arts du
Canada de son soutien. L'an dernier, le Conseil a investi 153 millions de dollars pour mettre de l'art dans
la vie des Canadiennes et des Canadiens de tout le pays. Ce livre est financé en partie par le gouvernement
du Canada.* We acknowledge the support of the Ontario Arts Council (OAC), an agency of the
Government of Ontario, which last year funded 1,737 individual artists and 1,095 organizations in
223 communities across Ontario for a total of $52.1 million. We also acknowledge the contribution of
the Government of Ontario through the Ontario Book Publishing Tax Credit, and through Ontario
Creates for the marketing of this book.

HOW A POEM MOVES

TABLE OF CONTENTS

INTRODUCTION

Here's something that makes me crazy: I know dozens of readers — smart, informed, enthusiastic readers of fiction and non-fiction of all kinds — who are afraid of poetry. Who fear they "don't get it." If you are one of these people, this book is for you.

I'm not going to try to make a case for why poetry matters. I'm going to just work from the assumption that poetry matters. It matters to me. It matters to the thirty-six poets included here. And it probably matters to you; if you don't think poetry matters, you wouldn't have bought or borrowed or stolen this book. So we'll leave the generalizations about poetry to others. Ultimately I can't say I get very excited about trying to define what poetry *is*. I'm more interested in what poetry can *do*. So while I'm not going to be afraid to get a little professorial if a term or technique needs some explanation or context, I'm going to do my very best to steer clear of big sweeping generalizations. We're going to dig in and get our hands dirty in the details.

The premise I'm working with is that, like a cookbook or a field guide, the best way to learn about a subject is to watch someone do it, so you can see that it's not as hard as it may seem, so you can start to do it yourself. The metaphor I like best is the enthusiastic park ranger. I may have a bit more expertise in seeing the flash of bouncing yellow in the distance and knowing it's a goldfinch. I'm familiar with the landscape and know good places to look for things. But my only job and hope is that I can show it to you so that you say, "Hey, I see it!" It's even better if, the next time you see that bouncing yellow in the distance, you'll be able to say to yourself, without me, "That's a goldfinch."

This project got started when I had the honour to serve as one of three jurors for the Griffin Poetry Prize for 2015. From November until late March 2016 I read over 630 books of poetry from all around the world and then discussed those books with my incredible fellow jurors, Tracy K. Smith and Alice Oswald. Seven of those books made it to the Canadian and International Shortlists. As the process progressed, I kept thinking, How can I make use of all this good reading? How can I shed light on some of these other books that aren't making it to the shortlists? There were terrific books that had to be put aside. Even uneven books often had stellar poems inside them. And I wanted to find a way to revisit them once the whirlwind of the jurying process was complete.

The answer I came up with is a blog called *How a Poem*

Moves, which has evolved into the book you now hold in your hands. There used to be a regular column in one of the Toronto newspapers called How a Poem Works, and I always enjoyed the format of short informal essays talking their way through poems, though I never liked the verb they used in the title. I like how art *moves* more than I like how art *works*. So for a year I posted an essay every two weeks, creating twenty-five entries. Most of those essays are now here, but I'll eventually get the blog running again, so if you are curious you can find it at https://howapoemmoves.wordpress.com.

The response I got to the blog was very satisfying. Of course the poets themselves were pleased. More than anything, poets want attention paid to their work, and so even if my treatment of their poems was not exactly what they intended when writing them, they appreciated my enthusiasm and care.

But most of my readers were of two types — first there were the poetry "insiders" who appreciated being introduced to a poem or a book that they hadn't encountered, or maybe seeing my reading of a poem they did know. The poets themselves fit into this category. If you are one of these readers, welcome. Many of you could probably write equally interesting essays about other poems, and I hope you will. I don't own a copyright to the format. For you, this book might serve as a sort of travelogue of my jury experience from 2015 — a "hey, did you see this?" My Canadian readers might have missed Diane Seuss or Natalia Toledo. American readers might have missed Jeff Latosik or Rahat Kurd. I've generally avoided the big names, who get more attention paid to their work elsewhere. And so if you haven't heard of many of the poets included here, I hope you'll have reason to find out more about them.

The majority of the blog's readers though were not what I'd call "professionals." They were the moms at my kids' school pickup line. They were students. They were colleagues from other disciplines. My mother. These people are serious readers who rarely pick up poetry because they are worried about "doing it wrong." If you fit that profile, thanks for joining me. I flatter myself to think that the project might provide a public service — not just for readers like you by giving you access to contemporary poems, but also for *poetry*, by giving it access to more contemporary readers like you. That's how the blog started transforming itself into a book.

I've started with four "background" essays about some of the first poems I fell in love with as I was learning about poetry. These are the oldest poems being examined here, though they only go as far back as the late 1980s. The last seven essays are about the books that were chosen as the finalists for the Griffin Prize in 2016. In between are twenty-four poems that range from the surreal to the heartbreaking, the dense to the breezy, the traditional to the experimental, the formal to the freakish. I did take some care linking essays about poems that have something to do with each other, so there is an arc if you care to find one. But there is not a curriculum — you are *not* required to read this book straight through. Feel free to skip, circle back, scan or skim. If you like a poem, read the essay. If you *don't* like the poem, read the essay and see if I can change your mind. You are not required to change your mind. You are not being graded.

One thing I tell my students all the time, and maybe it's a good place to end this introduction: don't worry at first about what a poem *means*. Meaning is only one of the things that a poem does while it's moving down the page. Instead ask, "What does the poem *do*?" This allows us to start off with some simple answers like, "It uses regular stanzas," or "It describes a scene with birds in it." This question also focuses us right away on the pleasures a poem provides. We don't watch an accomplished dancer and ask ourselves, "What does that dance mean?" We don't look at a painting and worry at first, "What is the meaning of that colour choice?" We might do some of that later, but our first response tends to be, "Wow." I'd like to get you to "Wow" with each of the thirty-five poems included here.

Okay, enough preamble. Let's get to it!

How a Poem Puts Skin on a Mystery

Philip Levine, "Making Light of It"

I was only seventeen when I started as an undergraduate at Tufts University, outside of Boston, but I already knew that I had literary ambitions. Hearing this, an upperclassman said to me, "You should take Levine's class, 'The Poem.' It's not supposed to be for freshmen, but he doesn't care. Come to a few classes and he'll sign you in."

So my friend Risa and I gamely attended while this gruff, brilliant, wiry man with a ferocious moustache brilliantly opened poems to us, interspersed with terrifying workshops and occasional rants about the Tufts administration, American politics, and dogs. "Levine" was Philip Levine, whose hard-nosed lyric poems earned him an international reputation, a cartload of awards, and a post as the Poet Laureate of the United States.

His class was a life-changing experience — he challenged and motivated me, a privileged kid from rural Connecticut, and opened a door to contemporary poetry that started me on a journey that I'm still on. I've saved an essay I wrote for him on which his sole comment was, "Some of this is quite sharp. Some dull."

This was the fall of 1987, so he must have been putting the finishing touches on *A Walk with Tom Jefferson*, which came out the following year and includes this poem:

Making Light of It

I call out a secret name, the name
of the angel who guards my sleep,
and light grows in the east, a new light
like no other, as soft as the petals
of the blown rose of late summer.
Yes, it is late summer in the West.
Even the grasses climbing the Sierras
reach for the next outcropping of rock
with tough, burned fingers. The thistle
sheds its royal robes and quivers
awake in the hot winds off the sun.
A cloudless sky fills my room, the room
I was born in and where my father sleeps
his long dark sleep guarding the name
he shared with me. I can follow the day
to the black rags and corners it will

scatter to because someone always
goes ahead burning the little candle
of his breath, making light of it all.

      — from *A Walk with Tom Jefferson* (Knopf, 1988)

  Levine's popular reputation is largely based on the hyper-realistic poems he wrote about factory work in his Pulitzer Prize–winning book *What Work Is*, but he always had a streak of surrealism in him too, built on a love of the Spanish poets from the period around the Spanish Revolution in the 1930s. This isn't the venue for a full exploration of Lorca, Vallejo, or Jorge Guillén, but when I return to "Making Light of It," it strikes me how Levine manages to switch back and forth between a gritty, no-nonsense portrait of the Sierras in California and something deeper, darker, and more mysterious.

  We begin with a speaker calling out a "secret name," but before we can wonder why he's calling, or who the angel is, Levine steers us into a clear-eyed description of the environment, landing us with the beautiful and perfectly tangible image of the dried out, wind-blown rose petals of late summer. "Yes, it is late summer in the West" helps to firmly locate us geographically but also serves as a helpful pause after the long, complex sentence that preceded it. Meanwhile, the relevance of the "secret name" hangs in the background — who is this angel who guards his sleep? Why does the speaker need to call to it? Is the call an acknowledgement or an entreaty?

  I want to point out a bit of music here that is one of Levine's unsung talents. Listen to the open sounds that happen as this first sentence comes together: the blOwn rOse links back to the light (like nO other) grOwing in the east, and later with the rOyal rObes shed by the thistle. As well, I count a full *nine L*s in that first sentence and a trio of *E*s (sEcret, slEEp, East). All of this alliteration and assonance, for me, adds to a ceremonial aspect of the poem — it is consciously *composed,* almost formal despite the plain language, and moves at a stately pace.

The lines that follow "Yes, it is late summer in the West," are all rich descriptions of the landscape — the tough, burnt fingers of the grasses, the royal robes of the thistle. The mystical import of the first line seems to have departed for a moment, while the speaker adjusts himself to his waking life in a specific, beautiful, but also punishingly dry landscape. But there's a progression there too: the matter-of-fact "Yes, it is late summer in the West," leads to the more elaborate description of fingers of the grasses and the royal robes of the thistle. The metaphorical leaps here are not out of reach, but they feel increasingly evocative, scratching at the mystical. Why would the thistle wear "royal robes"? Yes, they can be purple, but why would the poet evoke royalty in a plant that is so small and unassuming?

What I'm getting at here is how the poem is training us to make bigger and bigger leaps in our metaphoric imagination. All metaphors ask our brains to do some work, to make connections between two unlike things. Because metaphors are not explicit in *how* the connection should be made, our brains get the pleasure of making the connections themselves. If I use a simile like "Frank's as big as a house," you know exactly the parameters of my comparison — bigness. But if you say, "Frank's a tank," you are asking me to invent the ways in which Frank is like a tank. Of course size will be a part of this, but in the case of "tank," I might also think about hardness, unstoppable movement, and a potential for violence. Levine's personification of the plant life at this point in the poem sets us up for the magic that follows. So that when "a cloudless sky fills my room," we are prepared by the natural metaphors in the previous lines, ready to be taken by surprise by the fact that the cloudless sky that fills this room is not limited to the weather.

The last two sentences of the poem form an elaborate metaphor for the spirit of the speaker's father, who is sleeping "his long dark sleep" and also guards "the name that he shared with me." What is it about guarding and names? At the opening of the poem, the speaker uses a secret name to summon an angel who guards his sleep. At the end, his father guards the name they share. In both cases, the speaker seems spookily *cared for, looked after* by these spirits. He even has the freedom to "follow the day" as far as he likes, because "someone" (a third spirit? a living person?) continues to make light of his father's memory, "burning the little candle / of his breath." This image reminds me of the ceremonial yahrzeit candles Jews use to commemorate the dead. The candles give off little light, but last a long time, and are meant to provide a warm, lasting comfort to those who mourn.

I admit I'm not fully sure how the angel and the father's spirit fit together in the mind of the speaker. I'm also not sure whether the "making light of it" at the end of the poem is literal or figurative. Are the people who burn the candle of his father's breath making actual light of his memory? Or does he mean the colloquial "making light of it" that suggests that others dismiss the speaker's obsession? Does it have to be either one? Either way, I keep returning to the poem, reliving its mystery because it seems like a crucial discovery for the speaker, the way he understands his inheritance, and his place in the beautiful harsh world he lives in.

How a Poem Shapes Memory

Deborah Digges, "Stealing Lilacs in the Cemetery"

If Philip Levine was my first inspiration as a teacher, Deborah Digges was my first mentor, the first person at Tufts who took real care and time with my young slapdash poems. She was patient, learned, and, I must add, languorously gorgeous in a way that gave my still-adolescent heart a distinct, extracurricular thrill during our occasional one-on-one conferences. The central lessons I remember learning from Digges concerned the shape a poem makes — on the page, yes, but also in the mind as it travels across its subjects.

Stealing Lilacs in the Cemetery

for my son

> Down the lilac alley
> we picked stars
> > within stars, each cluster
> > > the one
> > thing among many.

> It was your fourteenth
> birthday, and morning
> > and Sunday. The lilacs
> > > were for
> > the table. I saw you

> watch me at a distance — I
> wished you
> > might remember me this
> > > way, stepping
> > toward you over

> the perfect squares of sod covering
> the new graves like
> > doors into the earth,
> > > my arms
> > full of flowers.

— from *Vesper Sparrows* (Atheneum, 1986)

The poem begins with a bit of sonic music ("lilac alley"), and moves quickly into some visual magic. "[W]e picked stars / within stars" is a visual description of the lilacs themselves but carries some vaguely biblical underpinnings ("wheels within wheels," from Ezekiel). And "each cluster" being "the one / thing among many" reminds me of *e pluribus unum*, a way of saying how we are stronger together. So we start with a precise, allusive voice, reflected in a meandering indented form that seems to mirror the leisurely walk the speaker is taking with her son.

Despite the fact that the title admits the mother and son are stealing, they don't seem too worried about any consequences. The poem is relaxed, careful, and the regular stanzas, with extra white space expanding the shape of the poem on the page, adds to a slower reading experience.

In the second stanza we get some useful information about a special occasion, and preparations for a party. But the poem's central shift occurs in the third stanza with the "watch me at a distance — I." The enjambment in that stanza is awkward, breaking an unwritten rule about how line breaks are usually built to call attention to an evocative word or image. The pause here feels tentative, a reflective shift in the speaker's mind from the image-based memory of the first two stanzas, to a more complicated emotional discovery. If her son is turning fourteen, our speaker must be aware that her days of wandering through a cemetery with him to pick lilacs are rapidly approaching an end. There's the immediate unspoken pull of a mother who knows her son will soon grow beyond her grasp. (We need a word in our language for pre-nostalgia, the awareness that a moment we are experiencing is special, fleeting, destined to cause us sweet pain when recalled later.)

But the speaker's mixed emotions are not just about how her son is changing, but also how *she* will change. She is aware of herself in this moment as being at her best: at ease, a bit mischievous, and still beautiful in the eyes of her son and herself. So she wishes her son "might remember me this / way" because she knows that this self will also change, fade. She has to be aware of all the less-flattering ways that sons remember their mothers. Keep in mind also that they're doing this bit of thievery in the cemetery, and she can't help but notice that they are surrounded by "perfect squares of sod covering / the new graves like / doors into the earth." No matter how many flowers you steal, in the end the cemetery gets it all back. So her desire for her son to remember her *this* way is about establishing a legacy for her son's memory.

Of course, by writing this poem, and by framing the scene so explicitly, Digges has slyly ensured that *we* remember her this way too. So the poem helps to fulfill the speaker's wish, inscribing in our memory an image of a happy mother and her son before whatever comes next for them.

Deborah Digges died in 2009, at fifty-nine, too young. And so my images of her are bittersweet, as I'm sure are those of her sons. But one of those images is unquestionably this one of her with an armful of pilfered flowers. I suspect that would please her.

How a Poem Articulates a Feeling

C.K. Williams, "Love: Beginnings"

C.K. Williams' *Flesh and Blood* was the first book that I carried around with me like a talisman. I did some backpacking in Europe in the spring of 1990 — although for some reason I never got myself a backpack and insisted on carrying a duffel bag thrown over one numb shoulder. I'd often be reading *Flesh and Blood* while walking on the side of some German highway, brooding on it, muddying its pages. There was something compelling in how Williams' poems capture very specific images or feelings, and his willingness to use prosy language and elaborate syntax in order to get it *precisely,* trusting that the situation, or image, or feeling, was evocative enough to sustain the weight of the extra verbiage. The poems in *Flesh and Blood* all follow the same form — eight long lines which can almost be read like prose, except they're too tight, too perfect. It's like prose at its very best, all the time. And the snapshot quality of the poems couldn't find its way into any other form.

Love: Beginnings

They're at that stage where so much desire streams between
   them, so much frank need and want,
so much absorption in the other and the self and the
   self-admiring entity and unity they make —
her mouth so full, breast so lifted, head thrown back *so* far in
   her laughter at his laughter,
he so solid, planted, oaky, firm, so resonantly factual in the
   headiness of being craved so,
she almost wreathed upon him as they intertwine again, touch
   again, cheek, lip, shoulder, brow,
every glance moving toward the sexual, every glance away
   soaring back in flame into the sexual —
that just to watch them is to feel again that hitching in the
   groin, that filling of the heart,
the old, sore heart, the battered, foundered, faithful heart,
   snorting again, stamping in its stall.
     — from *Flesh and Blood* (Farrar, Straus and Giroux, 1987)

There's no question that the language is prosy — the whole poem here is one sentence long, and hinges on an elaborate, almost legalistic, structure: "the stage where so much . . . that just to watch them is to feel . . ." Even cutting out all the asides and details that illustrate the "stage" he's writing about, it's still a sentence more suited to a textbook than an emotional outburst.

But let's not dismiss the music contained here: the few short lists about the couple's bodies are rhythmically compatible. The description of her body is based on a series of three-stress phrases ("mouth so full, breast so lifted, head thrown back") while the adjectives describing him each have one stressed syllable ("solid, planted, oaky, firm"). With its driving rhythm and suggestive language just on this side of appropriate ("firm" indeed!), we get a feel for the couple's almost embarrassing public display of affection. We've all seen these couples, and laughed at them with our friends. Get a room, kids.

But we also get a clear sense of the speaker's distance. Is "firm" really so risqué? While observing this lustful couple, our speaker is clearly *not* distracted by his *own* emotional situation. He is fascinated, but apart. His language is studied, searching for accuracy. The list of body parts (cheek, lip, shoulder, brow) is a bit prim considering the scene he describes, and while he refers to everything "moving toward the sexual," his own language is restrained, polite. The tone of the poem reveals that the speaker has more separating him from the couple than a higher sense of decorum. He is not a lovelorn compatriot mourning a recent breakup while eyeing another's happiness with envy. He is clearly in a different stage of life.

But even he is ultimately overcome by their passion and we get to witness it. That's why the ending, for me, is just transcendent.

First off, we've been waiting for it since the beginning — by now, the length of the one sentence has built up a momentum so that we anticipate, perhaps with a bit of impatience, a satisfying conclusion. We can see as we read that we're almost finished with the poem, but the "that" that opens line 7 arrives as the fulfillment of a kind of promise the grammar of the poem makes at its opening.

Then we get the speaker's admission about how the couple affects him. That phrase, "hitching in the groin," is so specific and odd that it feels almost the opposite of sexual. We can imagine our friend thinking to himself, "Ahem, what is that sensation I'm feeling? Yes, it's a sort of *hitching* down there, isn't it?" We can see how hard it is for this speaker to access the emotions behind the sensations. Or perhaps he's more interested in describing the feeling than experiencing it again.

Then at last even he breaks down. Notice also how early on in the poem the metaphoric moves are a bit scattered. The man is described as "oaky," the woman "wreathed upon him," but these plant images don't really feel connected. They are always "soaring back into the flame of the sexual" — but this metaphor too is fleeting, dropped as soon as it's spoken. Williams holds back the big metaphoric flourish until the end, when that most familiar and hackneyed of symbols — the heart, please not the heart! — takes on a new life in defiance of our embittered, calloused, cliché-exhausted eye.

Just as our poetic use of the heart *as a metaphor* has been overused and mistreated (by pop song, bad poem, pleading politician, and false advertisement), so too (we now realize) the speaker's old war-weary heart has been knocked around. But every once in a while, we encounter something in the world that gives rise to our need to summon it again. Our friend's reticence is broken down now — hell, he uses the word "heart" *three times* in those last two lines! Notice also how the piling on of adjectives from earlier ("solid, planted, oaky, firm") now gets redoubled: old, sore, battered, foundered, faithful. It's that last one, faithful, that kills me. The heart that, whatever its scars, still longs for passion, and is true. The last flourish, "snorting again, stamping in its stall," gives a wonderful, affectionate, and painful metaphor that brings the rhetoric of the magnificent lead-up into a hard-won transformation. The heart as a horse, safely stalled away, but still wanting to run.

I remember reading this poem as a twenty-year-old hitch-hiker hoping for an affair that would evoke the kind of language Williams uses here. Now, almost thirty years later, I am roughly the same age as Williams was when he wrote it, and I find myself having much more in common with the speaker. I too love observing a young couple's enchantment because it stirs in me the memories of that passion and self-absorption. And while I doubt that my wife of twenty-three years and I will be making a similar spectacle of ourselves any time soon, it's an intensity of desire I miss. This poem articulates that feeling exactly, and then gives me a metaphor — the horse, the heart — to bring it to life.

How a Poem Crystalizes an Image

Yusef Komunyakaa, "Yellowjackets"

It's clear already that I've been very lucky in my teachers, and Yusef Komunyakaa was another of those who crossed my path and widened it. Komunyakaa's reputation bloomed in the '80s and early '90s with the publication of a series of books including *Dien Cai Dau* (1988), a book of poems about the Vietnam War, and *Magic City* (1992), which draws material from his childhood in Bogalusa, Louisiana. After that, he won the Pulitzer in 1994 for *Neon Vernacular: New and Selected Poems.* This was right when I knew him — in 1992 I started working on my M.F.A. in Bloomington, Indiana, where Komunyakaa was teaching. So I got to witness Yusef's star go from bright to supernova.

As a mentor and teacher, Komunyakaa taught me an enormous amount about concision. I remember drafts of my own poems coming back with edits trimming syllables and small words (-ings were a particular problem). The idea, as you can see in "Yellowjackets," was to make a poem as compact as possible so that its imagery and music are as sharp and clear as a gemstone.

Yellowjackets

When the plowblade struck
An old stump hiding under
The soil like a beggar's
Rotten tooth, they swarmed up
& Mister Jackson left the plow
Wedged like a whaler's harpoon.
The horse was midnight
Against the dusk, tethered to somebody's
Pocketwatch. He shivered, but not
The way women shook their heads
Before mirrors at the five
& dime — a deeper connection
To the low field's evening star.
He stood there, in tracechains,
Lathered in froth, just
Stopped by a great, goofy
Calmness. He whinnied
Once, & then the whole
Beautiful, blue-black sky
Fell on his back.

— from *Magic City* (Wesleyan University Press, 1992)

"Yellowjackets" opens like a folk tale, with Mister Jackson's plow stuck in a stump that houses a swarm. The two similes in that opening — the beggar's rotten tooth, the whaler's harpoon — border on the humorous, the way folk tales often do. They also tend to hint at danger though: the beggar and the whale that are evoked are both capable of lashing out at those who disturb them. If this *were* a folk tale we'd probably follow Mister Jackson as he strives to retrieve his plow without too much pain or difficulty. There might be some elaborate, misguided scheme.

But this is not a folk tale. By the end of the first sentence, Mister Jackson is gone, and the rest of the poem hovers in the moment of calm, or of tension, while the horse waits for what's to come next. Meanwhile, the observing eye of the poet makes a series of images that are delightful but continue to escalate the tension until it breaks.

Let me back up one minute and talk about economy of language. The lines of the poem are relatively short and packed. They are also often enjambed — that is, they don't end where the punctuation is, so the comma in line 4 is in the middle of the line, while line two ends with "under," which forces us on to the next line in order to make sense of the phrase. All of these moves work *against* the folk tale style — a folk tale tends to be conversational and light, with asides and jokes. The poem here is deliberate, careful, and moves much less quickly than Mister Jackson did.

Also, adjectives are few and far between. In the first two sentences, there's "old" and "rotten," but the only other adjectives are there to tell us whom things belong to: a beggar, a whaler, and a "somebody." For a poem that's based so much on description (rather than action, or meditation, or whatever), that's not a lot.

Even the decision to combine "plowblade" into one word makes it a single noun rather than a noun with an adjective attached. Is this really a revision for the sake of a single space? I'd guess yes. (For non-American readers it's also usually "plough," can you imagine adding another whole *two letters*!)

The next three sentences, which spread over ten lines, all describe the horse from a safe distance. First, it's "midnight against the dusk," giving us a sense of time and light, but the fact that he is also "tethered to somebody's pocketwatch" is a delightful transformation of the contraption that is keeping him in this precarious position. The ticking of a watch might also remind us of the time he's running out of.

Nevertheless, the horse seems to exhibit a kind of composure in the midst of the crisis. He is contrasted to the disappointed women at the five-and-dime — he has a "deeper connection / To the low field's evening star." And, most delightfully, despite the fact that he is still sweaty from his work in the fields (the wonderful sound of "lathered in froth"), the horse now exhibits a "great, goofy / calmness." That word, "goofy," is such a tonal outlier in the poem that it fills me with affection for the animal. Is he just stupid, oblivious of the danger? Or is he some sort of foolish saint who accepts his fate with grace?

These images are all given to us during this moment of suspended tension, partially because of the seed planted in our head by the title — we *know* the poem is about yellowjackets, no matter how our attention may have been distracted. As clearly as we may come to see the horse, we must not forget the poem is not titled "Mister Jackson's horse." And so our knowledge of the abandoned creature being in a kind of danger is vivid, even as the narrator avoids the subject.

The final image is one that might frustrate a reader who wants a clear answer to the question, "Did the yellowjackets attack the horse?" There's an element of ambiguity here. The "blue-black sky" *could* be just the darkness, metaphorically described as falling on the horse's back because of his position at the top of the hill. We'd like to think that, for the sake of the animal. And if that's the way we read the poem, we are left with the horse both at danger and at rest, poised in stasis and funny in his precarious leisure. The image is beautiful and rich.

But we can also see that final image as a swarm of yellow-jackets so thick it is like the whole "blue-black sky" suddenly descending on the horse in one fell swoop. The image is terrifying, thrilling, and just as clear in the mind. So which is it?

Can't it be both? Can't we hold both possibilities in our minds simultaneously? Might that even be part of the pleasure of a poem? It's not a folk tale or a news report. We don't need to know what "really happened." If we can't decide, or if we can live with both explanations, then the image is beautiful *twice*. Personally I have grave concerns for the horse and, given the title, I suspect that the yellowjackets will make another appearance. But I can also treasure the creature at rest on the top of the hill, the picture of blissful ignorance. That ambiguity is one of the central reasons the poem has stuck with me for the twenty-five years since I first read it.

How a Poem Makes Meaning with Music

Elise Partridge, "Domestic Interior:
Child Watching Mother"

I love this poem first and foremost because of its exquisite music.
The dramatic situation of the poem is not hard to grasp, and the
average reader shouldn't be put off by its approach to its mate-
rial. But there's plenty here to sink your teeth into.

Domestic Interior: Child Watching Mother

Chapped hands sift greasy suds.
She can't make rent. Quietly,
she's crying again.

Vessels tip in the rack.
Each night I watch her eyes
to make sure they keep drying.

— from *The Exiles' Gallery* (House of Anansi Press, 2015)

The scene is set up immediately with the title, and in the first line it's clear the mother is washing dishes. Partridge is not trying to create any sort of mystery, and by the second sentence of the poem, "She can't make rent," we're introduced to a straightforward dramatic situation that doesn't require a lot of elaboration. The mother is stressed and sad, and the child is watching her. It's a set piece, a "domestic interior" like in a painter's study.

What makes the poem remarkable is Partridge's exquisite, careful musicality, and how that music propels us through the poem. In the first line we can hear the fizz of the dish soap in the sink with all the *s*'s in "hand*s s*ift grea*s*y *s*uds." So the sounds of the words used to *describe* the scene help us to experience it more sensually, with our ears and our mouths. Alongside these *s*'s are the short *a* vowels in "ch*a*pped h*a*nds," "c*a*n't," and "ag*a*in." (Partridge was an expat American, like myself, so I presume she'd pronounce the word "again" as rhyming with "men" rather than "main.") Almost all of the vowel sounds in this first stanza sound flat, cut off from any expansiveness by the sharp *t, p,* and *k* sounds that snap shut words like "chapped," "can't," "make," and in the next stanza, "tip" and "rack." Of course to some extent I'm superimposing my reading of the emotional content onto these vowels — vowels aren't inherently emotional. But again, because of the dramatic situation that Partridge has established so quickly, I'm encouraged to associate these sounds with my sense that the mother is trapped by her circumstances, that she can't find a way out, that even the alphabet is conspiring against her, that all she can do is continue to wash dishes, observed with concern by the child.

Keep an ear out for one other vowel sound in that first stanza though. "Quietly" and "crying" introduce us to a sharper long *i* sound that will reappear at the end.

If "Vessels tip in the rack" follows the same trajectory that has been established in the first stanza (sounds and description), something else seems to happen in the last two lines of the poem. First off, we turn our attention to the child's perspective of the scene, whereas in the first four lines we've focused more on the mother. Even a phrase like "make rent" from line 2 is probably the mother's, not the child's, but the final sentence of the poem is something a child might be able to articulate. We also get the first appearance of an "I" — this isn't just some random child watching her mother; the perspective zooms in and we begin to realize that the scene is a self-portrait for the poetic speaker, a memory.

The "I" also echoes those long *i*'s that we saw in "quietly" and "crying" above. Now we quickly get that sound four times in two lines with "night," "I," "eyes," and "drying." If you make those sounds in your mouth you can already feel that they are more open than the flat *a*'s that dominated the first stanza. I'm not going to go so far as to suggest that they form a layer of resistance for the speaker, that "drying" is somehow more optimistic than "crying" — that seems a bit much. The poem is still a dark interior, clouded by poverty and struggle. But in the only two-line sentence in the poem, as Partridge piles on more open vowel sounds like "each," "sure," and "they," perhaps the idea enters our mind that if the poet has grown to be able to recall a memory like this, and to write so carefully about it, she must have survived it.

There's a nice, subtle pun at the end with "make sure they keep drying," implying both that the child wants her mother to continue to dry the dishes, but also that she will continue to dry her eyes, that she won't give up despite her circumstances. And the crying/drying rhyme that gets summoned at the end also provides us with a witty philosophy of life that the child seems to have ingested — crying and drying, crying and drying, how else do we lead our lives?

"Domestic Interior" gives us a poignant snapshot of a childhood of worry, but also perhaps hints at some resources that emerge from that experience. Not just hardship, then, but struggle. It's a beautiful short poem, evocative because of Partridge's precise and discerning ear. Three books from her were not nearly enough.

How a Poem Snapshots a Moment of Drama

Tiphanie Yanique, "My brother comes to me"

My brother comes to me

They are at the red gate
of my grandmother's white house
The gate is taller than them both
The mother, who is my mother, is holding her son's hand
The boy, who is my brother, is only four years old
She, our mother, is going crazy
She wants to take him with her
A blood stain has spread permanently on my brother's white shirt

I am at the steps of the house, like a bride
I am fifteen and calling to my brother, "Come to *me*"
Her teeth are bared They are not pearls
"*I* am your mother," she shouts
We are all crying and all our tears are all different
Our mother's hair is a flame above us

— from *Wife* (Peepal Tree Press, 2015)

This poem moves very fast to describe a moment of such power and desperation that it seemed to me on first reading that I had missed something. At the centre of it all is a boy with "A blood stain" on his shirt. We don't know how it got there, and we don't exactly know why the women around him are acting the way they are. There's a power struggle between the speaker and her mother, and the conflict hinges upon a choice that the bleeding brother must make between them.

Of course, we know already what the boy chooses because of the title. Because it's the counterintuitive choice (wouldn't a bleeding child usually go to his mother before anyone else?) we search through the poem for clues as to why, what in the situation makes the boy's choice different from what we'd expect.

A couple of things about language to get us there. First, there are no periods but there are commas, quotation marks, and standard capitalization. I should mention that the history of punctuation usage is a surprisingly complicated one. Our rules for how to use capital letters, commas, and other forms of punctuation in poetry weren't "standardized" until the nineteenth century, and as soon as they were, some poets immediately started breaking them. Because the central purpose of punctuation is to help us in our reading (not, as you may have suspected, to make us hate high school English), poets often omit some of them as extraneous. Poets have line breaks to help with comprehension, and Yanique also uses regular capitalization to keep things clear. While it may look strange, the period-less sentences in this poem don't prevent us from understanding what is happening. Instead, the missing periods make the sentences fall over on themselves, increasing the speed of the reading, especially when the sentence breaks happen in the middle of the line ("Her teeth are bared They are not pearls").

We're also starting to sense something about the speaker by her matter-of-fact tone. Mostly she uses straightforward subject-verb sentences without a lot of excess detail. The gate is red, the house is white, the boy is four years old. She sees the gate and measures it against the height of the boy and his mother. She sees the shirt and knows the stain won't come out. What's emerging is a speaker who, in her memory at least, looks back with a ruthless, pained clarity on events that changed her life and the life of her family.

Then there's what's *not* being said, really the two most important things. First, what has happened to the brother? A blood stain on his white shirt could be from a nose bleed or a gunshot wound. We wonder, how desperate is this moment? A few lines later the two women are each trying to convince the boy to come to them, and if the choice is really his, then the blood must be from a wound less life-threatening than a gunshot. Still, the question hangs in our minds: how did it get there? Was it the mother? Someone else who is not in the scene? By cutting out the explanation and only providing the physical fact of the red stain on his shirt, Yanique leaves us with that question unanswered.

One quick thing about the word "permanently": it's the only four-syllable word in the whole poem, a jarring bit of over-explanation. Of course the word literally refers to the bloodstain on the boy's shirt that will probably not come out in the wash. But the word also reminds us that the scene itself, the terrible choice the brother has to make, will leave a permanent mark, both on him and on the woman recounting the story.

The second unanswered question concerns the mother "going crazy." The proximity of this line to the brother's blood at first made me think she is reacting to her son's injury, the way many mothers would if their child were bleeding. But when we see her teeth bared and that they "are not pearls," we start to wonder if the speaker means "crazy" literally. That would of course explain why the sister has, from the steps of the house, compelled the boy to leave his mother behind. The sneaky little pun on "going" works here because it seems that, wherever the mother is planning to take her son, it's clear they're also going to be going to "crazy."

But the sister, our speaker, is now daring to replace that mother: "Come to *me*" is not just a suggestion. It's the type of command a mother gives, which a child knows to obey. Meanwhile the mother's line of dialogue "*I* am your mother" sounds like the self-absorbed pleading of a disappointed adolescent. We have found the sister and her mother at the moment when they exchange roles. And the speaker's comparison of herself to a bride in the previous line makes it clear that she knows her situation is about to change, per-manently, as she takes on the care for her four-year-old brother.

How terrible for a boy so young to have to make a choice like this. How terrible for the girl, who must urge him to make it. And how terrible for the mother, whatever her madness, who realizes that she must release the grip she has on her son's hand in the fourth line of the poem — no four-year-old boy could break out of a mother's grip if she is not somewhat willing to let him go. No wonder they all shed their different tears.

We don't know what happens after the child goes to his sister, how the mother reacts, or how the family — sister, brother, grandmother — set about making lives for themselves in the aftermath. A poem doesn't have the same obligations that a story has to complete the narrative and show us what happens next. By honing in on this terrible moment of decision and change, Yanique gives us a vivid glimpse of three lives in crisis, with a complexity that continues to unfold into the unknown. That she does so in such a small space, with such plain language, is a remarkable achievement.

How a Poem Seduces Us with Outlandishness

Diane Seuss, "Free beer"

There are poems that are driven by narrative, by a story or situation. I can imagine a good short story writer creating a version of "My brother comes to me" in prose. Other poems lend themselves to music, or short films, or paintings. This is not to say that these poems are any less worthy, only that their subject matter is translatable across art forms. It's a fun mind game for me to think about the question, "If I were to remake this poem in another art form, which would I use?"

And then there are some poems, like Diane Seuss's "Free beer," that could only work as a poem.

Free beer

I'm the one who can hold a mouthful of salt.
Bring him here, the fool dressed in prison stripes.
I can pray for him, even though his eyes are wild.
I can de-louse the rat.

When I was a kid I invited them all to a puppet show.
There were no puppets; I'd planned no show.
Free beer, I said, and they came.

I've seen a puppet theatre.
It resides in the black cavern behind my eyes.
Thoughts are puppets, dangling from their tangled strings.
Bring him here, the one spinning on gloom's rotisserie.

I'll section an orange for the wretched bastard.
I'll ladle him up a mugful of tears.
Free beer, I'll say, though there is no beer.

           — from *Four-Legged Girl* (Graywolf Press, 2015)

Let me start with a quick technical thing: notice the stability in the formal aspects of the poem. Each line consists of one sentence, meticulously punctuated. There's no enjambment, and so each line functions discretely, as its own little nugget of thought. That helps keep things clear on the one hand, but it also allows Seuss to go just about anywhere from line to line — there's no necessary logic that demands she stay on one topic, no argument or narrative that needs completion. The clear grammar and stable form serve as the scaffolding for the roller coaster.

There appears to be a consistent speaker throughout the

poem, but we know she might say just about anything, from haunting truth to absurd lies. "Gloom's rotisserie" is now permanently etched into my mind as a vivid way to understand depression, but I'm hoping the image of delousing a rat (how — shampoo and a fine-toothed comb?) gets out of my imagination very soon.

The presumed "purpose" of the series of statements in the poem also seems familiar — a sort of invitation to us to "bring him here," and a kind of resumé of why we should bring our friend to her. But is it an offer to help someone who is suffering? Or an indirect seduction? Who is this poor fellow on gloom's rotisserie? And who are *we* to deliver him to this person who introduces herself in such a way?

If this were real life, we could be forgiven if we let this series of invitations slide to the bottom of our inbox. Our friend in his striped outfit could probably find more qualified counsellors. But let's not dismiss her too quickly, or gloss over the promises she makes. There is a hint of tenderness that shouldn't be underestimated amidst her more outlandish confessions. Sectioning an orange is something you do for a child, carefully and often with tenderness lest the sections break and bleed. And the best way to fill "a mugful of tears" is to produce them yourself, and so our speaker clearly has emotional similarities to our friend that perhaps we don't share. The surreal logic of it all starts to make a certain sense — only someone who can ladle a mugful of tears could possibly share our foolish friend's difficulties.

By the way, each time I type "gloom's rotisserie," I'm tempted to type "grief's rotisserie" instead, and as I turn the poem over and over again it seems clear that loss or loneliness is at the centre of the speaker's world as well as the object of her attentions.

What sort of person would choose to introduce herself to us primarily by reporting her deceptions? Who would describe her own mind (where her memory of a puppet theatre "resides") as "the black cavern behind my eyes"? Who would be so desperate for company that she would call out "free beer," even if there was no beer, like a delinquent version of the boy who cried wolf? And who would admit all these things to us and still beg for us to bring a friend to her so she might section him an orange and ladle him a mugful of her tears? Looking again, I see this poem as a desperate cry for connection.

It's also ridiculous, and the speaker seems vaguely unhinged. But tell the truth: part of what drew you to *this essay that you are reading right now about this particular poem* is "FREE BEER." See? It works! It's the outlandishness that makes it appealing. By the way, I have no free beer for you, nor (to my knowledge) does Diane Seuss or her publisher Graywolf Press. There is no free beer here.

But we do have "Free beer," the poem, the suggestion, the lyrical absurd half-story. And let's remember that the fourteen lines of this poem are not claiming to be real life, and therefore, *in the poem,* we are not required to behave responsibly. And so I say, *yes,* I've been waiting for someone capable of delousing the rat! Yes, I will attend your puppet show! Yes, I will bring my suffering friend to you so that you can carefully section him an orange. And whenever you say, "Free beer," I will be sure to come, because even if there isn't beer I'm certain there will be something else, something strange and inviting, a mugful of tears to baste me on my rotisserie of gloom.

How a Poem Cooks Up Dark Insight

Philip Metres, "Recipe from the Abbasid"

A common poetry classroom assignment is to write a "how to" poem, explaining some activity or recipe. It's often a fruitful exercise because it forces us to pay close attention to detail and invites us to think metaphorically about something mundane ("How to Tie a Knot"), or to think concretely about something more metaphoric or abstract ("How to Judge" or "Arson: A Recipe"). Here Philip Metres draws on a recipe found in Nawal Nasrallah's *Delights from the Garden of Eden: A Cookbook and History of the Iraqi Cuisine*. But aspiring chefs should probably go back to Nasrallah's original text before attempting to feed their families — Metres has made some rather unappetizing alterations . . .

Recipe from the Abbasid

Skin & clean a fat, young sheep & open it
like a door, a port city hosting overseas guests

& remove its stomach. In its interior, place
surveyors in exploratory khaki, a stuffed goose

& in the goose's belly, a stuffed hen, & in the hen,
machine gun nests, C rations, grenades, a stuffed

pigeon, & in the pigeon's belly, a stuffed thrush,
& in the thrush's belly, contractual negotiations

& subtle threats, all sprinkled with sauce. Sew the slit
into a smile, dispatch handshakes. Add Chevron,

Exxon, Texaco, Shell. Place the sheep in the oven
& leave until this black slimy stuff, excretion

of the earth's body, is crispy on the outside,
& ready for presentation.

— from *Sand Opera* (Alice James Books, 2015)

I should mention before I dive in that *Sand Opera* includes poems that are much more wide-ranging and experimental than the one reproduced here. The first section, "abu ghraib arias," is a mournful reexamination of the treatment of prisoners by United States servicemen and -women at the notorious prison of the title and at Guantanamo Bay, and includes text from a Standard Operating Procedure handbook, moving testimony from both Americans and former prisoners (some of it blacked out or partly erased), and texts from the Bible and the Code of Hammurabi. Other sections deal with Metres' own conflicts between his American upbringing and his Arab heritage and sometimes include such strange additional material as a floor map of a prison cell and a reproduction of Saddam Hussein's fingerprints. All of this, especially as it accumulates, has a lot of impact, and there's more to say about it all, but given the limits of my enterprise here, I thought it best to focus on something that can stand alone for readers. Please do go and check out the book though.

The metaphoric language as the poem begins appears at first to be in the service of vivid description — we are to open the sheep's skin "like a door," or perhaps like "a port city." These similes might be a bit elaborate for a standard cookbook, but given the medieval source (more on the Abbasids shortly) and the fact that we know we're reading a poetic rendering of the recipe, perhaps we should expect such leaps of language. I speak from experience when I say that overthinking the correlation between a sheep's internal organs and the structure of a port city is more fanciful than clarifying, but that doesn't mean it isn't intriguing.

Soon though, we are instructed to insert "surveyors in exploratory khakhi" into the interior of the sheep, and our metaphor-making has to change direction. For a brief amusing instant I admit I wondered if this was some culinary idiom — if we can make "pigs in a blanket" or a chow mein noodle "bird's nest," why not "surveyors in khaki"? But it doesn't hold up and we realize that it's the sheep, rather than the stuffing, that is becoming the metaphoric vehicle. We speed through historical tag-marks that point to European colonial rule (surveyors) to the Second World War (C rations and machine gun nests), and eventually to more modern representations of the "West": "contractual negotiations & subtle threats." All of this is clever enough for us to wonder what it is we are cooking, and we sense the ironic anger simmering under the veneer of hospitality. But this poem isn't merely an anti-colonialist screed; in fact it contains a much more far-reaching and complex critique of power and wealth.

From roughly 750 CE until the 1500s, the Abbasid Caliphate, based mostly in Baghdad, ruled a large section of what we now call "the Middle East," and presided over what historians now often refer to as the Golden Age of Islam. From the development of algebra to *The Book of a Thousand and One Nights*, the Abbasids were the epitome of an advanced civilization. Only a culture with significant wealth and expertise could conceive of a recipe that includes (if we stick to the edible parts) a thrush inside a pigeon inside a chicken inside a goose inside a sheep. On the one hand, it's glorious. On the other, it's absurd. And knowing how luxury has usually been built on the subjugation of others, it is easy to surmise that few in the Caliphate would have had access to the kind of delicacy referred to in this poem. The final line, "& ready for presentation," makes it clear that we who are cooking this fabulous meal are probably not going to partake in it.

One of the secrets to the Abbasid's success was its openness to the influence of other nations — particularly from Persia, but also China and elsewhere, East and West. So the lines "Sew the slit / into a smile, dispatch handshakes" seems to point the finger not just at the colonial power-brokers from elsewhere who exploited the region, but also at those who have been complicit in those efforts, welcoming them with traditional hospitality on the one hand, but an eye toward personal gain on the other.

So while the poem invites a familiar reaction against oil companies like Exxon and Shell, a closer reading reveals that rather than some sort of historical aberration, these corporations are merely the most recent in a series of powerful forces that have always exploited the region and its people, contributing to the suffering that in this poem is in the margins (although it takes centre stage elsewhere in *Sand Opera*) but also patronizing the craftsmen, artists, and scientists whose achievements might appear in a twenty-first century recipe book. Can we create luxury without oppression? Will it be ever thus? How much more must we shove into that pathetic, accommodating sheep?

One final note regarding tone. A recipe tends to be written in the imperative case: do this, mix that, bake for forty-five minutes. When we read these instructions we rarely find ourselves opposing them — "What do you *mean* I should preheat the oven to 350 degrees?!" But by the end of this poem, I find myself cultivating a kind of internal resistance, not just to the recipe itself ("No, I'd rather *not* add Chevron to my roast thanks") but to the whole enterprise the recipe now refers to. Of course, the poem doesn't provide an answer for *how* to separate the pairing of luxury and oppression. But by calling our attention to it, Metres encourages us to imagine a different recipe altogether that will feed everyone with generosity and taste.

How a Poem Pushes Us Away
and Beckons Us Closer

Marilyn Dumont, "How to Make Pemmican"

Marilyn Dumont's "How to Make Pemmican" is another recipe poem and uses some of the same techniques as Metres'. Again, there's something I like about how a "how to" poem forces us to be deliberate and specific. Also, the imperative voice used in a recipe (do this, do that) stands in fruitful contrast to most other kinds of poems.

But it's never enough to simply reproduce a recipe or instruction and call it a poem — there needs to be some sort of tension added to the directions. In Metres' poem, historical-political information is blended into the recipe to produce a surreal monstrosity of a meal. In Marilyn Dumont's "How to Make Pemmican," the tension is . . . well wait a second. I'm getting ahead of myself.

Marilyn Dumont traces her ancestry to Gabriel Dumont, one of the central figures (along with Louis Riel) who resisted Canadian authority in Manitoba and Saskatchewan in the late 1800s, just after Canadian Confederation. Her book *The Pemmican Eaters* explores aspects of Cree and Métis culture, retells episodes from the Riel and North-West Resistances, and challenges textbook versions of the history of Western Canada. Apparently the book's title comes from a term then prime minister John A. Macdonald used to refer to the Métis who were giving him so much trouble, but it seems to be a moniker that Dumont wants to reclaim. There's lots to learn about this period in Canadian history, and I am a novice here myself, but there are many resources out there about the Red River Resistance and Louis Riel that are worth exploring further.

I should also mention that it's a bit unfair to look at this poem on its own, out of context from the rest of Dumont's book. Like my discussion of Metres' "Recipe for the Abbasid," this essay only gives a narrow glimpse into what's going on in this wide-ranging and ambitious collection. But I hope it might serve as a doorway in.

Pemmican (from the Cree word for fat or grease) is a protein-rich combination of fat, dried beef (usually buffalo), and berries which was portable and didn't spoil, making it an important source of protein for travelling trappers and hunters in the nineteenth century, and for Indigenous Peoples much earlier. Nowadays it's championed by a wide range of enthusiasts beyond its Cree and Métis origins, including wilderness campers,

Canadian history buffs, and some spookier sites like Off The Grid News and Urban Survival Site: How to Survive in the City When Disaster Strikes.

All this goes to show that even a "simple" recipe for pemmican carries a lot of baggage with it. So to the poem:

How to Make Pemmican

Kill one 1800 lb. buffalo
Gut it
Skin it
Butcher it
Slice the meat in long strips for drying
Construct drying tripods and racks for 1000 lbs. of wet meat
Dry it while staving off predators for days
Strip from drying racks and lay on tarps for pounding
Pound 1000 lbs. of dry meat
Mix with several pounds of dried berries, picked previously
Add rendered suet

Cut buffalo hides in quarters
Fill with hot dried meat, berry and suet mixture
Sew quarter-hide portions together with sinew
Bury in a cache for later   mmmh.

> — from *The Pemmican Eaters* (ECW Press, 2015)

On the surface, there is nothing particularly attention-grabbing about this series of instructions. The language of the poem is straightforward, the lines clear despite minimal punctuation. Unlike Metres' "Recipe from the Abbasid," which spins off quickly into the bizarre, this one stays on task. One is tempted to blithely say to oneself, "With these instructions I could probably make pemmican too."

Except that you can't, because what's missing is *everything* — every line only leads to more questions. "Kill one 1800 lb. buffalo." How exactly does one set about doing *that*? Even a hunter with a lot more experience than myself might be hard-pressed to bag the type of animal Dumont so flippantly starts off with here. And if we somehow manage to kill one, how are we to gut, skin, and butcher it?! Perhaps I'm revealing myself to be a city mouse without much worldly knowledge, but I suspect that the majority of poetry readers are similarly inexperienced when it comes to buffalo butchering. So even the opening line of this recipe becomes a way to let us know that we're not going to learn how to make pemmican from a one-page recipe. There's a lot more to learn before we can even really begin.

This tone continues, with more slyly simple-sounding directions that open up further questions and challenges. What sort of drying racks hold 1000 lbs. of meat? How might one construct them? How does one pound that much meat? How does one render suet?

All of this makes this short poem a different sort of instruction. Because pemmican is so closely associated with the Métis, especially during the period with which the book is concerned, the implication is that we must understand pemmican in order to access the most basic aspects of Métis culture. However, obtaining that knowledge is going to require more work than we might have previously thought. A reader might wonder: If I can't even imagine the taste of this staple food, how can I possibly get inside the culture of the people who developed it?

On the other hand, you don't have to know how to make pasta from scratch to appreciate it. Ditto gefilte fish, tofu, or apple crumble. There's ultimately, then, an element of invitation here as well. To my ear, the speaker in this poem is saying: You know almost nothing about what pemmican is, but if you try harder, keep asking good questions, and then *listen*, you might be able find someone to show you.

But this poem is only the beginning. Partly I'm importing this tone from other parts of the book, but the assured voice here seems to indicate that if the next poem in the book was titled "How to Kill a Buffalo" (it's not), Dumont could list a series of similarly vexing, simple-sounding instructions that would lead us further in our study. I think of this mixture of rejection and invitation as one of the particular strengths of *The Pemmican Eaters*.

This is why that final "mmmh" at the end of the poem isn't just a throwaway line, or a taunt. It *is* a taunt, but it isn't *only* a taunt.

Quick explanatory tangent: My wife likes to watch cooking shows — *Chopped*, *Iron Chef*, and that *Chef's Table* program on Netflix that makes chefs look like the most fascinating and important people on Earth. I have very little patience for this genre of television, not because the people they profile aren't interesting, but because we never get to eat the beautiful food we are seeing. When we watch *The Voice* or *American Idol*, we can *hear* the emerging virtuosity of the singers. When (if) you watch *Dancing with the Stars*, the proof is in the performance, and if you know anything about dancing you can judge and (perhaps) appreciate a contestant's success right there on the stage. But there's always something crucial missing from the experience of these cooking shows. Maybe that's part of the appeal for my wife, leaving the final results up to the gustatory imagination. The "mmmh" at the end of this poem is a similar kind of tease. The speaker of the poem is letting us know that *she* knows the taste of pemmican, that *she* finds it delicious, that it's worthy of a hum of satisfaction for *her*. Those of us who have never tasted pemmican can't fully access the whole range of experiences, stories, beliefs, and cultural nuances that *The Pemmican Eaters* explores. However, it's also an invitation that the rest of the book attempts to make good on: if you'd like to know more, read on. By pushing me away (you know nothing about this), it also invites me in (come learn more). So in the end this poem/recipe is about confronting our ignorance. There's a challenge in it, and it requires a certain amount of humility to accept that challenge. But the rewards promise to be very tasty.

How a Poem Wrestles with Its Inheritance

Rahat Kurd: "Ghazal: In the Persian"

I've never been a big fan of the North American ghazal. There was a point a few years ago when it seemed that everyone was writing them, but I didn't find most of these manifestations particularly interesting. Or perhaps I could say that, for me, North American *adaptations* of the form didn't justify all the hullaballoo. For some poets, it seemed the use of the ancient form was merely a vehicle to claim access to an artistic tradition (with some post-colonial implications) that hadn't been deeply considered or adequately understood.

My friend Rob Winger disagrees with me, and he wrote a

book of his own ghazals *and* a fine essay for *Arc Magazine* on the subject. So, allow me to back away from big generalizations and get to the point of the matter, which is that my (perhaps misguided) reservations were temporarily tossed aside when I read Rahat Kurd's "Ghazal: In the Persian," from her book *Cosmophilia* (Talonbooks, 2015).

Rahat Kurd herself was born in Hamilton, Ontario, with Kashmiri Muslim ancestry, and it's fair to say that her relationship to her heritages — Canadian, Muslim, Kashmiri, Urdu — is a complicated one. There isn't space here to go into all of the issues that run through *Cosmophilia*, but they present a full range of responses to the position she inhabits in her linguistic, religious, political, and social world. Suffice it to say that the book does remarkable things by sitting "comfortably in its discomfort" when it comes to the traditions Kurd is playing with. She's not afraid to critique those traditions, but also continues to derive nourishment from them.

Skip this next paragraph if you already know about ghazals. If you don't, it's worth pointing out that they were developed in ninth century Arabia but were closely associated with Persian poetry from the twelfth century and with Urdu poetry in the nineteenth century onwards. In its traditional form the ghazal has a few very specific tropes (I'm mostly copping this list from Winger, so consider my ignorance only slightly clothed in others' knowledge):

1. A series of couplets that *don't inherently cohere* in logic or argument or narrative. This is one of its most compelling features.

2. There should be at least five couplets, and each tradition-ally uses the same rigid meter, chosen by the poet.
3. Each begins (at the end of the first two lines) with a refrain (or *radif*) that is subsequently repeated at the end of each couplet. In the poem here it's "in the Persian."
4. Because of this refrain, you end up with a rhyme scheme like this: *aa, ba, ca, da, ea,* etc.
5. The final couplet includes a pun or reference to the poet's name or pen name.

Kurd has mastery over all of these tropes (though the poem does not use regular meter) but applies them delightfully to an extended argument with herself about how uncomfortable she is in the tradition she is emulating. So, to the poem:

Ghazal: In the Persian

What secrets — and from me! — you kept in the Persian!
Rules beg to be broken as I grow adept in the Persian.

That love Faiz refused to give again, Lal Ded refused from the
    first.
Her fierce solitude sparks panic in every soul, except in the
    Persian.

Must it always be war when we meet? The times we meet are
    so graceful—
Your elegant farewells never falter, never ask me to return in
    the Persian.

I lost Urdu as I lost Kashmir, every time I left my beloved
women.
I found a circuitous way back to them, uphill, by stealth, in the
Persian.

They ask me, after such bitter loss, what possible consolation?
I tell them dry-eyed in the English: I know how Khusro wept
in the Persian.

The spy blunders most where he hoped to impress.
Licensed to kill it in Arabic! The joke's inept in the Persian.

The warmongers jeer: "Even the Taliban write poetry!"
But my improvised device pulls Sunni closer to Shia in the
Persian—

Listen: Shujaat Husain Khan weaves Mevlana in the sitar
strings of Hind;
Kayhan Kalhor bows his kamancheh's deep approval, in the
Persian.

As a serene heart? Rahat's *that* comfortable in the Persian.
As paradox? Being Rahat's *kheili mushkel* in the Persian.

　　　　　　　　　　— from *Cosmophilia* (Talonbooks, 2015)

One of the things the poem does is quickly introduce us to
a host of names, so that ignorant readers like myself can begin
to familiarize themselves with a rich tradition. It is clear the
speaker of the poem sees herself *within* that tradition even if
she doesn't feel 100 percent welcomed by it. The second couplet

refers to Faiz and Lal Ded, and by the time we finish I count five poets and musicians (plus Mevlana, a pseudonym of Rumi) who have been added to my to-read list.

But Kurd doesn't leave herself off the hook either, beginning her poem by admitting that the object of her affection has kept secrets from her in the Persian. She is slowly "grow[ing] adept in the Persian" but doesn't feel that she can make grand claims in it yet. Because of Persian influence on the form of the ghazal, and thus on Urdu poetry in general, a poet working via Urdu poetic forms must work her way "through the Persian." In the same way that a poet in the Judeo-Christian tradition will undoubtedly have to work through the use of imagistic parallelism that dominates the poetry of the Hebrew Bible, a contemporary poet in Urdu with any sense of her tradition must confront an inheritance that originates in Persia.

Who is the "you" in that opening line? "What secrets — and from me! — you kept in the Persian!" On the one hand, following one of the traditional tropes of the ghazal, it seems to refer to a specific lover (perhaps lost, perhaps fluent in Persian?) who has kept secrets from our speaker. On the other hand, ghazals frequently blur the line between a romantic addressee and a more mystical one. The "you" here could be the literary tradition itself, keeping secrets from our aspiring poet who wishes to imitate a form whose greatest works she cannot fully access because she can't read them in the original.

The opening couplet also lets us know that all of these issues can be addressed with a bit of humour. The odd way she offsets herself "and from me!" in the opening line is almost cartoonishly aggrieved (I'm hearing Miss Piggy's voice, "You kept secrets? From *moi*?!") and establishes a winking tone that serves Kurd well throughout the poem. This wit will also appear in the last couplet when she uses the phrase *kheili mushkel*. I had to ask Kurd herself to translate this. "Mushkel" means "difficult" in both Urdu *and* Persian, and "kheili" means "very," but *only* in Persian. So it's as if the poet has reached a point where, despite her continuing awkwardness with Persian, she recognizes there are things she can say only if she uses it.

What are we to do, inheritors of traditions we don't fully understand that often exclude or alienate us? How do we access their richness and virtuosity while still maintaining a healthy contemporary skepticism about their origins in other languages, other times, other value systems?

Here's what Rahat Kurd's poem seems to suggest:

1. Study the tradition. If you need to, name-drop the originators of fourteenth century (like Lal Ded) to the innovators of the twentieth (like Faiz). Use your form with virtuosity and wit.

2. Acknowledge the distance. Make your refrain "in the Persian" so that every time it repeats, we are reminded that the form, the situation, and anything that can come from your efforts are seen through the gauze of an imperfect understanding.

3. Then do it anyway. Despite, because of, and alongside these qualifications, doubts, and misunderstandings, make the poem into a baroque allusive delight using all of the nuances of the form at your disposal. Do your damned best to create an "improvised device" that is so powerful it can pull "Sunni closer to Shia."

4. Derive pride and nourishment from your efforts to

honour your inheritance, your acknowledgement of your imperfect gumption, and finally from your willingness to bend that tradition in order to conform its tropes to your own outlook and experience.

Does that seem like a lot to ask of an eighteen-line poem? Yes it does — which is why this one strikes me as so accomplished, even if I don't have access to all the information it contains. I ride through it feeling like I must put up signposts to return to later, but also with a growing sense that I know the feelings she is referring to, in a slightly different context and register — that is to say, in translation.

How a Poem Lives Between Languages

Natalia Toledo, translated by Clare Sullivan,
"Flower That Drops Its Petals"

If you are going to build a homemade hand grenade, you'd better
do everything exactly right. Better not to do it all than to do
it imperfectly. Most things aren't like that though. Good trans-
lation necessitates a compromise between the demands of the
original poem and the demands of its new language. There are
always changes, losses, compromises. But just because there's no
such thing as a perfect translation doesn't make the efforts of
translators pointless. On the contrary, the effort to bring a poem
into a new language can add to the readership of a fine poet and
also create something entirely original in its new linguistic home.

Frost once quipped, "Poetry is what gets lost in translation," but that may just be because he didn't do much translating himself. He certainly read his fair share of them, with pretty decent results.

Natalia Toledo is a well-known Mexican poet who writes in Zapotec, an Indigenous Mesoamerican language spoken by roughly half a million people, mostly in southwestern Mexico. There are plenty of resources to learn about the history and grammar of Zapotec, as well as some of the efforts attempting to preserve it. But if you just want a quick taste of what it sounds like, you can hear some online, including two poems in the voice of Toledo herself at the World Literature Today website.

Toledo translates the poems herself into Spanish, and in 2015 Phoneme Media published a book of American Clare Sullivan's translations into English, which includes Toledo's original Zapotec as well as the Spanish versions. Sullivan has the good fortune to be able to consult with Toledo about the origins of the poems. But the poems are still translations of translations, and so we are always seeing them through an opaque screen, trying to fathom the nuances we are missing.

For those of us who can't read or speak Zapotec, we must ultimately approach the poems as poems *in English*, echoing or reflecting Toledo's intentions rather than mirroring them exactly. The reflection will be naturally warped, but if our translator does well, then the warped reflection will have its own beauty, intention, and meaning. So let's have a look:

Flower That Drops Its Petals

I will not die from absence.
A hummingbird pinched the eye of my flower

my heart mourns and shivers
and does not breathe.
My wings tremble like the long-billed curlew
when he foretells the sun and the rain.
I will not die from absence, I tell myself.
A melody bows down upon the throne of my sadness,
an ocean springs from my stone of origin.
I write in Zapotec to ignore the syntax of pain,
ask the sky and its fire
to give me back my happiness.
Paper butterfly that sustains me:
why did you turn your back upon the star
that knotted your navel?

— from The Black Flower and Other Zapotec Poems
(Phoneme Media, 2015)

One of the things I love about this poem is the mix of the strange and the familiar, and how Toledo brings us along from one to the other. The lyrical tone of the speaker at the beginning ("I will not die from absence") is firmly in the romantic tradition — my first reading assumed the "absence" that she refuses to die from is the absence of a lover, and I don't think that reading is ever fully dispelled, although other more complicated readings are added to it. So as a reader I begin with recognition.

The other familiar tactic in the opening lines is the reliance on the natural world to illustrate the speaker's distress — "a hummingbird pinched the eye of my flower" is not an image I've encountered before, but the precision of the description, wild as it is, makes a kind of poetic sense. I'm not exactly sure what "the eye of my flower" is either, but with "my heart" in the next line, I can make an educated guess. Or to be more exact, I'm comfortable being in the *vicinity* of knowing what she means.

But things gradually get stranger as we move through the poem. I know what a curlew is (think of a sandpiper, with a long, curved, thin bill), but the idea that curlews somehow foretell sun and rain is new and odd, and I'm beginning to wonder if the speaker's "wings trembl[ing]" is such a bad thing. The references to the creatures in the speaker's home landscape are not only illustrating her distress, they seem to be providing her with the tools to resist it. So, after the repetition of "I will not die from absence," my sense is that "a melody bows down upon my throne of sadness" seems to be a positive development, as does "an ocean springs from my stone of origin." The way I read it, the power and fecundity of the ocean is going to help her fight off that potentially lethal absence.

By the way, here's something I often catch in English translations of Romantic languages — the frequent use of the construction "the XX of XX." In the tiny bit of Spanish I know, and a bit more in French, the words *del, de, de la, du* are so ubiquitous as to be almost invisible, the way we don't notice if the word "the" occurs a lot in an English sentence. In English we tend to notice that construction after a few instances, so that "eye of my flower," "throne of sadness," "stone of origin," and "syntax of pain" call attention to themselves a bit as Toledo's imagistic technique. I sympathize with Sullivan's challenges as a translator here though, because if you replace those phrases with "flower eye," "sadness throne," or "origin stone," it would sound a bit too clipped, brutal, abrupt, or Germanic for the general lyric tone of the poem. But I thought I'd point it out as an interesting way that bringing a language into English presents the translator with unique difficulties. I suspect this wouldn't be true with a translation from Spanish to French.

Meanwhile I want to know more about this "stone of origin," because if an ocean springs from it, it's clearly a source of bounty and assurance for our speaker. The mention of Zapotec in the next line supports the growing sense I have that this poem isn't really about romantic heartbreak, but rather about some sort of cultural alienation. Why is writing in Zapotec a way "to ignore the syntax of pain"? Knowing that Toledo also speaks and writes in Spanish, we can deduce that Spanish has a painful syntax, no doubt partly because of the history of oppression and violence that speakers of Zapotec faced (and continue to face) in the language, laws, and sentences of Spanish. But the idea that the very *syntax* of Spanish is painful is larger and more profound, because we ourselves are reading the poem via a Spanish translation. And we know that Spanish syntax has infiltrated into Toledo's own mind and mouth. (Most speakers of Zapotec, like Toledo herself, also speak Spanish in order to function in the public sphere.) She is a contorted person, in pain, in the syntax of Spanish, which she must use in order for us to understand her.

But Toledo's speaker refuses to perish under this, and because she has access to her native language, her declaration that she writes in Zapotec seems to be a way of explaining herself to outsiders like us, but also a way to work her way back to a language in which she can pray to "the sky and its fire" for happiness. Even through the double-gauze of two translations, we sense that the phrase that Sullivan has interpreted as "the sky and its fire" is likely a traditional one in Zapotec, perhaps with religious connotations. If her life in the broader world has forced her into a syntax of pain, this poem — and the others written in her first language — are her way back to the spiritual sources of her power and happiness.

The last sentence is mystifying in a way that delights me. The poem addresses some version of what we might call the speaker's soul, metaphorized as a "paper butterfly." But what is this paper butterfly? Is it a species of insect familiar to the region, or a reference to origami, an art form that must have been imported? And while the admonishment that she should not have turned her back on her heritage is one I've seen in other contexts, the image that illustrates it is again deceptively cross-cultural. "The star / that knotted your navel" seems to refer to both pre-Christian religious beliefs but also to more recent scientific discoveries about our origins in stardust. By reclaiming Zapotec, Toledo seems better able to live in and understand both the ancient and modern worlds.

Here I also want to give credit to Clare Sullivan for summoning the wonderful phrase "knotted your navel," which feels like a new way to illustrate a birth metaphor that is cultural more than it is biological. It also has a wonderful bit of alliterative music that is not in the Spanish ("que anudaba tu ombligo") but that I sense is there in the original: "beleguí biliibine xquípilu'." You don't have to be able to know how to pronounce that phrase to see all of the *b*'s and *i*'s playing off each other. So we have Clare Sullivan to thank for giving us a sense in English of what it might sound like for a Zapotec speaker to return to her language and culture in a way that will in turn help her face the world.

How a Poem Invites Us to Praise

Ross Gay, "Ode to Drinking Water from My Hands"

Odes are songs of praise, to a person or an event or an object — a wedding poem, or epithalmium, is a kind of ode, as are a lot of nature poems. Often, an ode can be a way to meditate on what makes the subject worth praising, so the topic can be less direct than the title implies. For example, the way I read John Keats' "Ode to a Nightingale," the real subject of praise is how we lose ourselves (briefly, fleetingly) when encountering something truly beautiful. You could say the nightingale is a vehicle for the poet's praise of that feeling of losing oneself.

The great twentieth century Chilean poet Pablo Neruda wrote a series of odes in the early 1950s that are some of his most plain-spoken and accessible poems. If you've had trouble getting past the lush surrealism of Neruda's love sonnets or the more epic scope of his *Canto General*, the odes are a great place to start. Partly motivated by a political desire to speak to (and on behalf of) common people, Neruda wrote odes to mundane things like "Ode to My Socks," "Ode to Broken Things," and "Ode to the Tomato," praising their usefulness and lack of pretention but also elevating their commonness by focusing his lyrical attention on them. The poems are also full of whimsy and joy and often a bit of nostalgia. He expresses regret that we have to "assassinate" the tomato to enjoy its freshness, and wonders at how his clothes "make me what I am" and vice versa. A teacher of mine once remarked that Neruda wanted to eat the world, and there's something boldly loving in these poems that is only matched in my reading experience by Walt Whitman.

I mention Neruda because he's clearly one of the presiding spirits for Ross Gay's *Catalog of Unabashed Gratitude*, the book from which this poem is drawn, and which contains a number of odes and praise-songs. The impulse to praise the simple and straightforward, even perhaps a socio-political desire to elevate the mundane by focusing poetic attention on it, is similar in both poets. But there are also some interesting points of departure. For one thing, Gay's odes are mostly about *actions* rather than *things*. Neruda's tomato, clothes, and yellow bird become Gay's "Ode to Sleeping in My Clothes," "Ode to Buttoning and Unbuttoning My Shirt," and here, drinking water with his hands. I want to explore this difference, but first here's the poem:

Ode to Drinking Water from My Hands

which today, in the garden,
I'd forgotten
I'd known and more
forgotten
I'd learned and was taught this
by my grandfather
who, in the midst of arranging
and watering
the small bouquets
on mostly the freshest graves
saw my thirst
and cranked the rusty red pump
bringing forth
from what sounded like the gravelly throat
of an animal
a frigid torrent
and with his hands made a lagoon
from which he drank
and then I drank
before he cranked again
making of my hands, now,
a fountain in which I can see
the silty bottom
drifting while I drink
and drink and
my grandfather waters the flowers
on the graves
among which are his

and his wife's
unfinished and patient, glistening
after he rinses the bird shit
from his wife's
and the pump exhales
and I drink
to the bottom of my fountain
and join him
in his work.

— from *Catalog of Unabashed Gratitude*
(University of Pittsburgh Press, 2015)

If you've perused any of Neruda's odes, you can see right away that the form here is a direct imitation/homage — the short lines, the straightforward language. The form forces us to slow down, but not in a way that feels pretentious. To me it reads more like the deliberate, present-tense wandering of the imagination as it connects back to memory. The act of drinking from his hands, which the speaker does "today, in the garden," reminds him of his childhood when he first learned this skill from his grandfather.

A little side note about those first few lines: he's telling us he's *forgotten* these things (drinking from his hands, being taught how) as a way of telling us that he's now *remembered* them. Just a neat little reversal as we go along, especially because it's not only the skill that he's now remembering.

So back to the question of actions versus things. In this poem, and in the other odes I've seen by Gay, the action being praised isn't significant in and of itself. This is in contrast to Neruda, who seems to want to elevate the subjects of his attention, in part just *by virtue* of his attention. This is a little unfair to Neruda, but I get a vision when reading his odes of all the little items of the world — marbles, pieces of string, dead mice — waiting outside his study hoping for him to bestow his poetic attention upon them. And that he would make time for them all if he could. Neruda's vision (like Whitman's) is all-embracing, and a little self-important.

Gay's odes, on the other hand, don't presume any kind of universalism. When he praises "drinking water with my hands," there's no presumption that this activity is as meaningful for everyone else as it is for him. (Notice how all of the titles of the Ross Gay odes I mentioned above include the word "my." They are intended, without apology, to be specific to his own experience.) Drinking water with his hands today, in his own garden, reminds the speaker of his own grandfather watering graves — "mostly the freshest," but also his own — and it's that *reminder* that makes the action worthy of praise. The action calls forth a whole host of feelings of grief and love, not to mention the sensual memories that get brought up with it — the sound of water coming up the pipe "like the gravelly throat / of an animal," or the "lagoon" that appears in his grandfather's hands. I love that word "lagoon," how it evokes the massive size (in the speaker's childhood memory) of his grandfather's hands. These memories and feelings are what's really being praised.

Weirdly, by focusing on an activity that is meaningful in his individual way, Gay's efforts feel welcoming, open to participation by us as readers. Instead of a line of little items waiting for Neruda's attention, I get an invitation: "This is how drinking water from my hands is meaningful for me; what simple actions are meaningful in this way for you?" I don't personally have any strong memories connected to drinking water out of my hands, but reading this poem I'm reminded of cracking my knuckles with my own grandfather, holding up my hand to his to measure its size, and am tempted to write my own "Ode to Cracking My Knuckles," to participate in a dialogue with Ross Gay. So the poem evokes not just his own memories, but summons similar ones in a total stranger — no small feat for a praise song. What might your memory be?

How a Poem Answers Some Questions but Not Others

*Amber McMillan, "The Light I've Seen in Your Hair
I Have Found in My Own Hands"*

This poem made me think about categories of mystery. Readers who are not comfortable with poetry tend to feel they don't "get it," partially because they're looking for the kinds of answers that many poems refuse to provide. Another way of saying this is that poems tend to solve different kinds of mysteries than fiction does. You'll see what I mean in a minute. Here's the poem:

The Light I've Seen in Your Hair I Have
Found in My Own Hands

I still hear rumours about the dead fox
we found nailed backward and upside down
from the rafters of Jenny's tool shed
at least three or more summers ago.
The rusted nailheads, its entry wounds,
were tucked from view beneath the slim
lip where the roof meets the open air.
It did not occur to me then we were stealing.
The jury-rig of the undiminished memory,
tripped up by emergency, is the steady
nursing of the conditional — the tedious
combinations of all possible outcomes.
That summer I told you *no* instead of *almost*.
I should have said *very very close*.

       — from *We Can't Ever Do This Again* (Buckrider Books, 2015)

McMillan starts with a pretty clear description: a dead fox that the speaker and a companion discover grotesquely displayed in Jenny's tool shed. The speaker's attention gets close enough to the animal to pinpoint where the rusty nails have been hammered into place. Most readers wouldn't say this part is confusing, but there are plenty of unanswered questions: who did this? Why? Was it an act of mischief or threat? How did the speaker feel about it, apart from fascination? And why is she still hearing rumours about the fox years later?

Some of these questions we might be able to figure out with some careful rereading: the rumours are probably connected to the "who did this?" question, which apparently has not been answered. The fact that people are still talking about the event three-plus years later reminds us of what a singular, cruel act it was, but we already knew that from reading the description. The persistence of the rumours also lets us know that the speaker is still connected to it somehow.

But then things get a bit stranger. "It did not occur to me then we were stealing." Does this imply that the speaker and her companion took the fox from its perch in the rafters? Is that what they were "stealing"? That would explain her attention to the nails in its fur. But why would this be considered stealing? Perhaps they did it without Jenny's knowledge? Did Jenny mind? The situation, at first a bit dark, now seems downright weird. Poor Jenny and her tool shed!

All of this I would call "narrative mystery," the confusion that we have when we're trying to figure out just what's going on in a poem or story. Novels and movies use this kind of mystery all the time, of course, to propel us through the action, and the eventual clarification of the mystery is one of fiction's pleasures. In genres like detective fiction, you could argue it's the *chief* pleasure. But a poem is under no obligation to solve narrative mystery — the uncomfortable situation with the fox hanging in the shed, and what the speaker did with it, is dropped, because it turns out the fox is only a trigger in the poem for a different subject altogether.

I'm going to skip the next sentence for a minute and go straight to the end. "That summer I told you *no* instead of *almost.* / I should have said *very very close.*" From a narrative standpoint, we suddenly understand why the speaker has brought up this memory: she's rethinking her relationship to "you," the person being addressed in the final couplet, who must have been with the speaker when she discovered the fox.

But now we're back to mystery: *what* should she have said "almost" or "very very close" *to* instead of "no"? If this were a novel or a story, we'd need to find out the details, but in a poem, it's enough to know the emotional repercussions of the "no." For me, the implication is romantic, or sexual — I'm imagining a range of questions for which "no" and "almost" and "very very close" are logical but also important answers: Probably not, "Do you have enough cash to buy my car?" More like, "Are you ready to get married?" or "Do you love me?" or "Do you want to sleep together?" Whatever the question was, her answer changed the relationship forever. If she had told her companion that she was very very close to saying yes, then the no wouldn't have seemed so final and everything would have been different. We can project a whole series of events that might have followed. We could write this story, though it wouldn't be as compact or as arresting as the poem is. So while we don't solve the narrative mystery exactly, the emotional mystery is clarified. We're in the realm of memory, regret, and curiosity.

This returns me to the previous sentence, the most complicated one and the one that, when I first read the poem, I blew past without retaining a lot. If I've referred here to narrative mystery (what's happening) and emotional mystery (how does the speaker feel about it), here we have something more like logical mystery (what's she saying?). Let's unpack the sentence and see:

> The jury-rig of the undiminished memory,
> tripped up by emergency, is the steady
> nursing of the conditional — the tedious
> combinations of all possible outcomes.

We have an "undiminished memory" that's been "jury-rigged," patched together from the materials at hand. Already that's odd — if the memory is "undiminished" then how has it been "jury-rigged"? The way I understand it, the memory of the fox has been jury-rigged to the emotional memory of the failed relationship. The speaker knows that linking the two episodes is "the steady / nursing of the conditional," a way to continue wondering about other "possible outcomes." Even if her imagination keeps finding them "tedious," she keeps going back, picking the scab, jury-rigging the memory.

I'm not sure what emergency "tripped up" the memory again for the speaker, but it's clear that it's not the first time this strange moment with the fox carcass, a memory she cannot push out of her mind, has become linked to the memory of a crossroad summer that could have ended differently. The poem becomes about what can't be undone: the fox can't be reanimated, the relationship can't be recovered. And now too the mistreated fox carcass is irrevocably connected to a woman's memory of a romantic near-miss, a time when a slight change of tone might have led to a completely different future. Her acknowledgement of the weird artificiality of that linking — the jury-rigging — is the toughest part of the poem to break open, but it is also the part when the poet emerges to give us a wink about what she's done.

This is a thing poems do a lot that fiction rarely does. If it's true that poems often don't have time to clarify *narrative mystery*, and sometimes force us to work awfully hard to understand *emotional mystery* and even *logical mystery*, they are much more open to revealing *artistic mystery*, the acknowledgement of how a poem works. Strong poems like this one are willing to point to their own scaffolding, like a magician who is so good at what she does that she can explain the illusion while she performs it, and we are still amazed. She can't separate the two memories in her mind, but now, neither can we.

How a Poem Clarifies Its Blur

Jeff Latosik, "Aubade Photoshop"

The speaker of Jeff Latosik's "Aubade Photoshop" is rehashing a relationship that has broken down, and the fault is at least partly his own. His desire to replay events, even to revise his memories of what's happened, leads him to some complicated syntax and metaphors. But they will also ultimately lead him to a hard-won nugget of insight.

Aubade Photoshop

That you might rope a past vacation's sky
whose blue was not that well expressed,
hog-tie its gaffes and vacancies, drag it
to a place between that time and this.

Not quite plucked from the invisible spectrum
like galaxies bright as cellophane in Quality Street
or happened into suddenly like a lapsed god's eye
staring back from light-year stacks of helium.

I could let a scrim of Red Label tint an afternoon
where things would give up shape and focus
and disclose, from a secret blush, all those vapoury proximities
so that shoals of my living and dead float up,

and all I said or didn't say in tune with hindsight's
unflappable A440 will be resaid, the way
it's easier to be right once the moment's fled
or how you expanded the range of your voice by aping Bocelli.

It was all just settling, lime stain on stone, or an ism
of which you've grown especially fond. Things I couldn't detach
but didn't know it yet. I had to write this as a kind of letter.
We put a screen in front of things to see them better.
    — from *Safely Home Pacific Western* (Goose Lane Editions, 2016)

Latosik's oblique title starts us off with a pun: aubade and
Adobe. Adobe, of course, is the company that makes and sells
the computer program Photoshop that many use to manipulate

images, whether cleaning up "imperfections" in a magazine cover or adding a missing family member into a group shot at a wedding. An aubade is an old poetic form, going back to the 1600s at least. It's a morning poem, traditionally spoken by a lover who must depart. (My personal favourite is John Donne's "The Sun Rising.") There's often regret, delightful longing, and a bit of a sense of danger or pressure on the speaker. Why does the lover have to leave? Is the affair illicit somehow or is it just the workday calling? Sometimes there's also the more metaphoric sense that our times of pleasure on Earth are fleeting, that the approach of death itself is like the harsh approach of dawn. Modern versions (like Philip Larkin's "Aubade") often follow the metaphoric path more explicitly, turning the romantic aubade into a meditation on mortality.

But what, then, is an "aubade Photoshop"? Even before we truly begin, Latosik introduces a conflict: "Photoshop" is a tool we use to control how and what we see, but "aubade" reminds us of our limitations. So how does this conflict play out?

We begin with the speaker musing on the power of image manipulation — the "that" that opens the poem is a shortening of a conditional construction like, "As if you could . . ." So, I could paraphrase (brutally) the opening stanza as something like, "As if you could change the background tone of the sky into something you'd seen before while on vacation . . . " What's strange is that it doesn't seem that the speaker wants to *perfect* his memories: the sky from the "past vacation" was "not that well expressed," and he wants to capture its "gaffes and vacancies," not its pleasures and fulfillments. So already the usual notion that we use Photoshop to improve our images seems turned on its head.

The next stanza lets us know that he's not seeking something beyond the ordinary — not from the "invisible spectrum," although it seems he's more interested in narrowing down his choices (not this, not that) than in expanding them. Latosik uses language from quantum physics (helium can be used to measure the heat of stars; please don't ask me how), but also refers to Quality Street chocolates, which are wrapped in brightly coloured — and easily differentiated — cellophane. What's emerging is the speaker's desire to put things in distinct categories, to clarify the messy shadings that make up his life and to simplify them into more easily interpretable primary colours.

He muses in the next stanza that he could accomplish something like this if he drinks enough Red Label whisky to put a "tint" on everything he sees and remembers. The impulse to want to put a different perspective on a situation (even by getting drunk) seems familiar and reasonable, but by now I'd guess you're wondering: Why the dense language and roundabout syntax? Why is the speaker taking such elaborate care to explain how he would like to see more simply and clearly? The desire for clarity, for tonal perfection (A440 is "perfect A" above middle C used as the tuning standard), is presented in a way that feels murky, filled with qualification. Our speaker is demonstrating, even when *saying* he wants clarity, that he can't achieve it. But why?

We get a hint when we finally see a glimpse of the "you" this poem has been addressed to all along. We learn two things about this friend at the end of the fourth and beginning of the fifth stanza: s/he has a talent for vocal parody and an attraction to isms. The first detail shows us that the addressee of the poem can have a bit of fun while still improving his skills, expanding his vocal range. (I'm going to assume the addressee is male for this reason — a woman wouldn't expand her vocal range nearly as much by aping Bocelli as she would by aping, say, Jessye Norman.) The second detail shows us that, unlike the speaker, the friend can do what our speaker cannot — he can see clearly, even if the ism he grows fond of is only a temporary solution. Because what is an ism (communism, feminism, existentialism, Judaism, etc.) but a way of clarifying our sense of how the world works? So the person being spoken to is adept at doing exactly what our speaker has been tying himself into grammatical knots expressing his *inability* to do.

And now that we finally have another person in the poem, the context of the aubade returns. It appears that something has gone wrong between our speaker and his Bocelli-imitating friend. He's painfully wishing that he could revisit their argu-ments ("it's easier to be right once the moment's fled"), but just as important, he can't reach out to his friend in person but "had to write this as a kind of letter." (Notice that even the categories "letter" and "poem" are blurry for our speaker — it's not a letter it's a "kind of letter.")

The final line, then, "We put a screen in front of things to see them better," works on a number of levels. First, it's finally a moment of simple statement, in a straightforward iambic rhythm, and is the only line of the poem that contains, and is contained by, a complete sentence. So it seems that the loss of the relationship, if not the relationship itself, has finally taught our speaker to make a clear truth claim. Let's call that progress.

Second, "We put a screen in front of things to see them better" is an admission of fault, a recognition that in his desire to see things better, our speaker struggles to categorize them more neatly than perhaps he should. We want to see things more clearly, and so we put barriers to our understanding of them, losing some of their complexity and nuance. But "see them better" could also mean "better than it actually was." The sense of nostalgia, of reluctance or longing that often permeates an aubade, is here turned into something like a desire to remember something more fondly. Maybe our speaker is finally realizing that the friendship wasn't all that great to begin with. And finally the last line points to the poem itself, a screen of language that seems to be gradually helping our speaker to come to terms with what he's lost. Forcing light through the screen of hydrogen gas helps reveal its chemical makeup. And forcing a complicated feeling through the screen of a poem might help clarify it as well.

How a Poem Changes As We Read

Ali Blythe, "Shattered"

The thing I like best about this poem is how it changes as I read it, so I don't want to say anything as a prologue, except I already have by telling you that I love how this poem changes as I read it.

Shattered

Your eyes look like
beach glass fresh
from a pounding.

I wish I could float
you inside an empty
bottle and raise your

many tiny sails.
But one has to accept
the tense of a feeling.

You will never be
well enough again
to exist on anything

but a diet of thin ice.
You will recurrently
have the sense someone

is checking the time,
which you suspect
might be suspended

from nurse-clean clouds
by a delicate gold chain.
You will have to drink

meds from a plastic
cup. Next, you won't
remember a thing.

— from *Twoism* (Goose Lane Editions, 2015)

When I started reading this, I thought it was a love poem, and it's not an unreasonable first response when it opens with a simile about eyes. Even when Blythe undercuts the potential romanticism with "fresh / from a pounding," I'm not sure where he's going — it could be a brutal sexual reference, or a bit of tonal misdirection. But I'm also aware, as I'm sure you are, that when sea glass is sufficiently "pounded" it ends up smooth and almost soft to the touch, and its colour washes out. So after the first stanza, my imagination is holding these possibilities in suspension, waiting to see where the poem is headed.

The second stanza doesn't exactly help, but rather introduces an even more elaborate metaphor: "I wish I could float / you inside an empty / bottle and raise your // many tiny sails." It's a wonderfully evocative image, but I'm still not sure what it signifies — something about how the speaker wishes he could open the addressee's full potential? Then why the boat inside a bottle? Does the speaker think of his friend as constrained in some way? Or is this something about preservation? We're going to find out in a second, but before Blythe clarifies it all, I want to pause a moment to appreciate how, by structuring the poem with these images — the sea glass and the bottle-boat — at the beginning, *before* the situation is explained, Blythe gives us a chance to bounce all sorts of possibilities around in our minds first. For me, that's a major pleasure, but these decisions also add to a mood of confusion, or of being off-balance, that hovers over the rest of the poem, even once the circumstances are made clearer.

Oh, and one more: what is the "tense of a feeling" that "one needs to accept"? Are all feelings only in the present tense? Can you have future feelings?

By the fourth stanza, then, a reader could be forgiven for being almost ready to give up on "Shattered" as too esoteric or self-referential, using imagery that only has meaning to the speaker. This is when Blythe pivots, at the exact centre, and things start to come rapidly into focus. Notice how flat and prosy the language of the next sentence is — "never be / well enough again / to exist . . ." almost sounds like a doctor's awkward formality, the line breaks slowing us down even more, and the images from the first stanzas continuing to leave a bit of a shimmer on the language.

So now we know that the speaker is visiting a dying friend or loved one. Suddenly my understanding of the sea glass from the first stanza zeroes in on the faded colouring, and the "pounding" from that opening sentence seems to refer more to disease (or perhaps its treatment) than to any of the other possibilities I was toying with. The boat bottle might have something to do with suspending time rather than other kinds of entrapment. And the "tense of a feeling" — well, I'm still not 100 percent sure about that one, except that even grammatical "tense" is now painful to the speaker because he knows that his loved one has no future.

Once we're on surer footing with regard to the "plot" of the poem, Blythe can go back to the image-making at which he excels. The speaker ventures into the mind of his companion, who senses those around her "checking the time." The image resonates because the patient must be acutely aware of when her visitors are preparing to depart her bedside, but also of the more ominous ticking down of her own life's clock.

By the way, I'm using a feminine pronoun for the patient and a masculine one for the speaker/visitor just for clarity since there's no indication of gender or even of the exact relationship between the two figures. This kind of ambiguity works in a short poem, but for readers of fiction it can be a bit frustrating — we're almost always aware, when reading a story, about the relationship between characters. But in a poem we sometimes only get "the tense of a feeling," stripped down to its bare bones. Because Blythe doesn't have time to explore the complications of the relationship here, he leaves it out. We only have feelings, images, and impressions. (Other poems in *Twoism* explore angles on loss that I believe are connected to this poem, and that form a composite from which we can extrapolate a bit more, but that's a subject for a different essay.)

As the poem makes its final turns, the sentences take on a parallel structure (You will . . . You will . . . You will . . . you won't), but they also get shorter and shorter, with ominous connotations. Also, the flight of fancy with which our speaker enters into his friend's imagination (time suspended from "nurse-clean clouds" by a "delicate gold chain" could be a medically induced hallucination) quickly shrinks down to the narrowest of perspectives ("drink // meds from a plastic cup") until at the close of the poem she vanishes altogether.

A clever grammatical move here is that these last four sentences are all in future tense — you will, you will — but they point toward a future that doesn't contain the friend at all. The final reference to remembering is a painful act of separation. Only the speaker will be able to look back at these moments he has described. His friend will be part of the past that he is now remembering.

This realization is what connects the glass images at the opening of the poem to the circumstances the poem describes, and also to the title which unites them: "shattered" describes glass that can never be put together again, but "shattered" is also a feeling, in the irretrievable present tense. I return to the beginning of the poem as if revisiting the moment when the shattering begins.

How a Poem Will (Not) Save Us

Raoul Fernandes, "Life with Tigers"

Life with Tigers

A rooftop will do in a town
with no cliffs. A Friday night
with cheap Merlot and a cheaper
radio will do. The wind
stirs, faint skunk then honeysuckle.
She tucks her arms and head into
the front of her T-shirt to light
the joint. I picture a cloud of smoke

between her small breasts.
Her shirt, stretched and faded,
says *Save the Tigers* across it. But
there are no more tigers left
on this earth. We smoke on the edge
of the roof, sneakers dangling. Crackling
music from a time and place
we've never been. It will do. The day's
heat still holds to the shingles.
She's lying on her back, looking up,
saving tigers. *Don't tell her,* repeats
in my goddamn head. Don't tell her.

    — from *Transmitter and Receiver* (Nightwood Editions, 2015)

At first glance this reads like a sweet if awkward seduction poem. The speaker (presumably male) finds himself on a rooftop in a city without cliffs, feels mild contentment in his surroundings ("It will do"), admires his female companion while she lights up a joint, and warns himself not to tell her that the desire expressed by her T-shirt (*Save the Tigers*), and whatever efforts she may have engaged in that pursuit, have been in vain.

The first question, then: why not tell her about the tigers? Likely the speaker believes that he is protecting her from the pain or disappointment of learning the truth. He wants her feeling good about her commitment to saving the tigers, even if all that commitment amounts to is the money she spent to purchase the shirt (probably a long time ago, seeing as the shirt is "stretched and faded"). Presumably he also wants her feeling good because the likelihood of a successful romantic consummation of the evening ("it will do") is predicated on her good spirits. So he's a nice guy, it's a nice evening, he doesn't want her to be sad, and he knows that she's much more likely to kiss him if she doesn't feel sad.

If that's all the poem is, it's still an evocative little bagatelle in a collection that fairly often portrays a speaker whose sensitivity is the defining feature of his character. But I believe there's more going on, making this poem darker and more interesting than this first reading suggests.

Let's go back to our first question then. Our speaker says, "there are no more" tigers left on this Earth. Last time I checked, this wasn't actually the case. That means one of two things: either the world of the poem is a fictional one, slightly in the future or in a skewed imaginary present, in which tigers are extinct; or it means that the speaker is wrong.

If the speaker is just confused, then frankly he's not worth our further consideration. A well-meaning simpleton, or a severely uninformed pothead who doesn't know that tigers still walk the Earth. *Google "tiger," doofus.* So let's leave that possibility aside. Although the after-effects of this line of thought, even once I dismiss it, make me read the poem with a bit more suspicion of the speaker as we continue. I'll come back to this.

The more likely answer is that the world of the poem is one that is slightly skewed, or slightly in the future, in which tigers have indeed gone extinct. The deliberate enjambment of "But / there are no more tigers left / on this earth" seems to support the idea that our speaker takes this fact very seriously and knows it well. So then I find myself returning to the beginning of the poem, trying to find out more about this damaged world in which there are no tigers. What else is different? If it seems normal enough on the surface (people still go to secluded rooftops to smoke pot and/or have sex, there is still the smell of skunk and honeysuckle, radios still exist and stations still play old music . . .), what else might have gone astray?

It brings me back to the first sentence: "A rooftop will do in a town / with no cliffs." My first reading above of this phrase suggested something like, "If your city can't provide a natural way to find a nice view, a rooftop will suffice." But then why "cliffs" specifically? Why not "mountains" or "hills" or even "scenic viewpoints"? The mention of cliffs always connotes the possibility of danger — you can *throw yourself off* a cliff. You don't throw yourself off a scenic viewpoint. So now I'm beginning to wonder about the usage of "will do," which occurs three times in this short poem. A rooftop will do *for what?* For a romantic encounter or a suicide pact? Is it "will do" as an expression of contentment, or an expression of impact sufficiency?

And what does our companion think of all this? Doesn't she know that tigers are extinct? Does she really care much about them in the first place? Maybe it's just an old T-shirt she got at the vintage clothing store. In fact the woman in this poem is hardly more tangible than the tigers are. The feminist romantic reader in me grows impatient — she has no agency and never speaks. She is unquestionably an *object* of affection, with a merely physical presence — she has small breasts, she's adept at lighting a joint against the wind, she sits down in sneakers, she lies on her back. But we have no idea about her real mind or emotional state. We can probably presume that she came to the rooftop willingly with our speaker, that they have some sort of friendship. But her one defining characteristic — that she wants to save the tigers — seems built on very flimsy evidence indeed.

So then we turn back to our speaker's flawed state of mind.

What seems crucial in the poem's process is not whether the woman wants to save the tigers ("She's lying on her back, looking up, / saving tigers." No, obviously she's not), but that the speaker *believes* she wants to save the tigers. He needs to believe she is. Moreover, it seems just as important that — in the speaker's "goddamn head" — there *are no tigers*, that the woman's efforts are doomed to failure. And finally, it's crucial to the speaker that his ability to withhold this information from his friend is what can save the evening from devolving into despair. Our speaker has invented a whole world for himself in which his friend is idealistic but vulnerable, he is worldly-wise but protective, and that the sum of this "will do" to keep them both from falling off the edge.

So instead of a quaint portrait of an awkward young man's inner monologue as he remarks on a pleasant romantic evening, the poem becomes a dissection of the series of acrobatic self-justifications he must use in order to convince himself that he shouldn't throw himself off the roof. The title, after all, is "Life with Tigers," so the poem lives in a state of denial of some of the very information it contains. If the poem is about "life with tigers," then the speaker is trying to will himself into his companion's (perceived) ignorance so that they can both lose themselves and not think of the darker edges that are closing in. But they are closing in, and we can't help but know it.

Did Fernandes intend all this, or am I giving the poem unearned credit for undermining its own assertions? The fact that I'm not 100 percent sure speaks either to Fernandes' sleight of hand or to my own ability to invent a lie to protect myself from jumping off the building of this book. But *Transmitter and Receiver* often articulates a sense of the precarious, of trying

How a Poem Loves a Misunderstanding

Richard Siken, "Dots Everywhere"

An ekphrastic poem responds to a work of art in some way. Often, there is a description of the piece (usually a painting) that puts its images into some other context. But that isn't necessarily the case. Sometimes the painting is a jumping off point for the poem, or a point of contention. A lot of poems in Richard Siken's *War of the Foxes* could be called ekphrastic. But Siken is a painter himself, and often his subject seems as much about the *creation* of an image or painting as it is about our response to viewing it. I know of other poets who were also visual artists (William Blake, first and foremost), but Siken is the first poet-painter I'm aware of who delves so deeply into the problems of creation, whether that creation is on paper, canvas, or in the imagination itself.

Dots Everywhere

I erased my legs and forgot to draw in the stilts.
It looks like I'm floating but I'm not floating.
Sometimes I draw you with fangs. I tell you these
things because I love you. Some people paint
with whiskey and call it social drinking. Some people
paint drunk and put dots of color everywhere.
In the morning the dots make them happy. I am
putting dots of color everywhere and you are sleeping.
Something has happened in the paint tonight and
it is worth keeping. It's nothing like I thought it
would be and closer to what I meant. *None of it is
real, darling.* I say it to you. Maybe we will wake up
singing. Maybe we will wake up to the silence
of shoes at the foot of the bed not going anywhere.
— from *War of the Foxes* (Copper Canyon Press, 2015)

The first thing I respond to here is the unsettling emotional context. Our speaker admits to occasionally imagining his loved one "with fangs." I imagine the image is probably not one the lover would find flattering. On the other hand, our speaker claims that he's reporting this vision "because I love you." I suppose that in some ways honestly divulging one's nightmares about one's partner is a good thing? If the poet-artist has also severed his own legs, and wants to tell his partner about that as well, perhaps this sort of dark sharing is a regular part of their relationship?

There's some fun to be had projecting this couple's regular dinner-table conversations ("How did you imagine me today, darling?" "With porcupine quills"), but for me there are important questions about the creative mind that are involved in this exchange. Can our imagination incriminate us somehow, especially as it's expressed in art? How much of what's churning in our brains do we need to take responsibility for? Is altering the way we experience reality damaging to the reality we are portraying?

Before a simple answer comes too quickly, the poem proceeds with a clever counter-argument: the speaker reminds us that "Some people paint / with whiskey and call it social drinking." The deadpan tone sounds like social commentary but is really an idea about perception — that some of us, by applying alcohol to our body chemistry, deliberately alter our perception of the people and situations around us. We think of this as "social drinking," and it doesn't seem like such a great sin. So what about changing our perception of others using color, as art often tries to do?

A brief aside about the "dots of color" that are referred to a few times in the next lines, as well in the title. It's hard not to think of Georges Seurat, the French post-Impressionist painter who developed pointillism and is best known for *A Sunday on La Grande Jatte*. Siken's description of the speaker's works in progress — with erased legs, people with fangs, etc. — makes them much more surreal than anything Seurat conceived. And from what I've read it's unlikely Seurat painted much while drunk. So I doubt Siken is referring directly to Seurat here as a subject, but Seurat's development of pointillism was based on contemporary scientific ideas about color perception. That is, he was very conscious of creating a vivid deception for the eye to enjoy.

There's a point, then, in lines 6–11, where the poet-painter-lover seems to be content riding his distorted inspiration, applied while his lover is sleeping, whatever the implications. As he reports it, "Something has happened in the paint tonight and / it is worth keeping. It is nothing like I thought it / would be and closer to what I meant." These lines will sound familiar to any artist, poet, or musician who has been happily led to new territory by an inspired mistake or tangent. Of course, the line is also somewhat deceptive — how can something happen "in the paint"? And how can the speaker know what he "meant" to accomplish if the painting that fulfills that intention is also "nothing like I thought it / would be"? The misperception of the *paint* moving the creative process forward — or the alcohol, or the romantic tension, or whatever — is part of how this painter convinces *himself* to move forward with his art. Misunderstanding seems crucial to the endeavor.

By the time we get to "*None of it is / real, darling,*" I sense that Siken is talking not only about the painting, and not only about the poem itself, but also about the whole nature of perception. The sentence sounds partly like a Katharine Hepburn quip and partly like Caliban from *The Tempest*. ("Be not afeard; the isle is full of noises, / Sounds and sweet airs that give delight and hurt not.") The idea seems to be that we can make ourselves crazy trying to discover what is "real," but we're much better off being content with the misperceptions that delight us.

Of course, our painter's creative success won't necessarily solve the romantic tension in his house. "Maybe we will wake up singing" feels promising, if unlikely. But "Maybe we will wake up to . . . shoes . . . not going anywhere" immediately summons the counter-image of the shoes going *somewhere*, leaving, stomping off, whatever. Maybe, maybe not. Love sits uncomfortably with creative inspiration: on the one hand, the artist's multicoloured visions of his lover are partly what fuels his love and creativity. But his pursuit of those visions, and their occasional brutality, also seem to have widened a gap that the poem struggles to bridge. Embracing the strange and surreal may help in the pursuit of art, but that doesn't make an artist easy to live with. This poem seems to acknowledge that problem with a wry grin, showing a bit of fang.

How a Poem Mistrusts Its Idols

Cassidy McFadzean, "You Be the Skipper, I'll Be the Sea"

You Be the Skipper, I'll Be the Sea

This time of year, Agamemnon's
tomb is swarming with Beliebers.
If I was your boyfriend, Clytemnestra . . .
What's the theme of this one, teacher?

We raised our iPhones in the dark
like gold-leaf masked talismans.
Our ringtones were a Greek chorus
calling from the hive to lion guards.

I'm a novel with the pages uncut.
Someone flipped me open and had enough.
Now reading me rips me in two.
What's a poem for? What's it to you?

Whoever said size don't matter lied.
The shaft of the cistern in the hillside
had me on my hands and knees.
I lapped up clay with my teeth.

We were catamarans in my last fantasy,
skipped in this world like a stone over sea.
You stole me away from the treasury.
Freedom, Siri, was a machine.

          — from *Hacker Packer* (McClelland and Stewart, 2015)

Cassidy McFadzean's shimmering debut *Hacker Packer* dances between scholarly travelogue and a skewed but loving embrace of popular culture. Underneath the playfulness, however, there are more serious matters at stake. It's easy to get distracted by the fun, but in "You Be the Skipper, I'll Be the Sea," the speaker has some serious concerns about love, power, and the imagination.

The poem finds us at the Tomb of Agamemnon, among the ruins of Mycenae, taking in a scene with the incongruous combination of guidebook information and contemporary technological accoutrements common to tour groups. McFadzean blurs the two influences on her experience so that Justin Bieber's seduction song is directed at Clytemnestra and the gathering of tourists becomes something like the fans at a concert, holding up their iPhones in an act that feels more about worship than it is about light.

Some brief background: in Greek mythology and literature, Agamemnon is one of the kings enlisted to help return Helen from Troy. He assembles his fleet but for days there's no wind. A priest finally tells Agamemnon that he must sacrifice his daughter Iphigenia in order to get things moving and he does so. Ten years (and many adventures) later, Agamemnon returns home (with treasure that includes the Trojan priestess Cassandra as a concubine), but his wife Clytemnestra has not forgiven him and, with her new lover Aegisthus, kills Agamemnon in the bath.

So if Justin is singing to Clytemnestra, is it in the voice of Aegisthus, pledging to treat her (and their offspring) better than her husband did? Or is it in the voice of a younger Agamemnon, making promises he will not keep? Either way, it's unclear if our speaker approves. The last line of the stanza, "What's the theme of this one, teacher?" suggests that like us she's trying to figure out what this combination of impressions signifies. And who is this teacher? Is it a question for a tour guide? A playful wink to her travel companion? Or a recognition of us as readers, hovering over her shoulder, tempted to educate her?

For some further background, I refer you to Justin Bieber's "If I Was Your Boyfriend," which includes lines like "Baby, take a chance or you'll never know."

You might also be aware that Justin Bieber, famous since childhood for his sweet voice and man-boy persona, has run into trouble for some of his more outrageous antics, including vandalism, dangerous driving, and assault. In other words, Bieber and Agamemnon have some things in common. They are both deeply flawed, larger-than-life male figures who attract our attention and admiration despite (and even partly because of) the wrongs they commit. Theoretically Agamemnon's military prowess and his loyalty to his male compatriots outweigh the damage he does to the women who rely on him. And Bieber's physical attractiveness, wealth, and fame outweigh his sophomoric destructive misdemeanors. Can we learn about the standards of masculinity in cultures from which these "heroes" emerge?

But back to the poem. In the second stanza McFadzean has some more fun conflating the contemporary worship of a celebrity like Justin to the worship of a warrior king like Agamemnon. The iPhones like talismans, ring tones like a chorus. In the hands of a lesser poet, this comparison, and the fun implications that can be made from it, would suffice. The poem would end there. But out of nowhere the third stanza starts with what looks like another quotation. You could be forgiven for assuming, on first reading, that these three lines are more Bieber lyrics. But they're much darker, and as far as I can tell, they're not cut-and-pasted from any other source:

> *I'm a novel with the pages uncut.*
> *Someone flipped me open and had enough.*
> *Now reading me rips me in two.*

The references to a book with uncut pages puts us somewhere historically between Agamemnon and Bieber. And the imagery, as well as the near-rhyme of uncut/enough evokes the kind of heartbreak (with implied sexual violence?) that poets have used, from Edna St. Vincent Millay's "Renascence" to Yeats' "Leda and the Swan." Is the speaker of these italicized lines the same one who is now at Agamemnon's Tomb? Or is she referring to some other story or poem? Either way it suggests that our tourist has turned her focus away from the attention-getting men and is thinking more about those who pay the price for their behaviour. And the stanza's closing line: "What's a poem for? What's it to you?" continues the train of thought that first emerged with, "What's the theme of this one, teacher?" The question of what impact the poem might have, and the challenge to an interpreting "you" (who, me?) is now something close to defiance and resentment.

In the fourth and fifth stanzas things are changing direction very quickly, and the sentences are disconnected, seeming to refer to a few things at once. Is the "size matters" comment really about ancient water systems? Is McFadzean using a phrase like "had me on my hands and knees" deliberately in order to evoke images of sexual submission, despite the fact that she seems to be refer-ring literally to exploring the site? Is the fantasy of catamarans skipping over the sea connected to the sacrifice of Agamemnon's daughter, or is it a romantic image of two lovers sailing together on their lives' voyages? And most disturbingly, by admitting that "You stole me away from the treasury," is the speaker connecting herself to Helen and Cassandra, to a legacy of sexual violence that persists even in contemporary pop lyrics?

The declaration at the end, "Freedom, Siri, was a machine," feels like a final turn in the screw. On the one hand it seems to imply that the way to get freedom is to procure a machine. (Imagine an advertisement for Harley-Davidson with that cap-tion.) On the other hand, the sentence can also be read as a way of saying that "freedom" is merely another kind of machine, that it won't necessarily protect us from the dangers present in the poem. The clincher of course is that it's addressed to Siri, another semi-mythological machine with imperfect answers for our questions. Siri cannot provide us with companionship or love, nor will Siri leave an archeological footprint that tourists might explore millennia from now. Or has Siri been the companion we've been talking to all along?

We are left with a sense that McFadzean's speaker is overwhelmed by the legacy of hero worship that can build magnificent tombs, launch global celebrity careers, and develop oracular technological tools, but cannot protect women from abduction or girls from their fathers. If she has a chance to find a way out it's through her ability to make insightful connections between the disparate stimuli she encounters, and a shape-shifting, penetrating wit that has a reader delightfully off-balance throughout the poem.

How a Poem Doesn't Dish

Damian Rogers, "Ode to a Rolling Blackout"

Ode to a Rolling Blackout

Teachers in Oklahoma seek to stop students
from discovering the gateway of digital drugs.

We're all having a hard time, but some problems
are preferable to others: the problems of the very rich,

for example. Some swear the pile is the only known
enemy of the hole. O pretty girls tripping on night,

enjoy this next round, as your pupils pour out
past last call. One of you will soon stop caring

for your hair and your delicates will start to sour.
You will pick your teeth clean with your coke nail.

Now you crackle like a coal, lips slick with petroleum.
Little pots of hot pink clink like crystal as you travel

down the black tube toward morning. Did you kiss
the devil's ass in the alley? Please, no more questions.

— from *Dear Leader* (Coach House Books, 2015)

I want to start my discussion about this poem by saying
something about near-confession, or half-confession. If you
don't know about the so-called "Confessional" poets from the
middle of the twentieth century like Robert Lowell, Sylvia
Plath, John Berryman, and Anne Sexton, there's plenty to dis-
cover. What these poets all have in common is a willingness to
plumb the depths of their personal experience, even at the risk of
revealing uncomfortable or embarrassing information. Lowell's
ambivalence about his family's legacy of privilege and dysfunc-
tion, Sexton's mixture of anger and passion about family and
womanhood, Plath's self-accusing romance with death — all of
these, at the time, crossed barriers about what could or should be
written about in poetry. Ultimately the most successful "confes-
sions" expand into something wider and more essential. That's
one reason why we continue to read them.

Despite what literary scholars and theorists have been telling
us for decades, it's still a common natural impulse when reading

lyric poetry to look for the poet's authentic experience in the subject matter. Knowing that Plath, Sexton, and Berryman all committed suicide adds a certain aura of authenticity to the anguish in their poems. But are poets under any obligation to deliver this kind of confession? Can we still be moved by a powerful poem about, say, a father's death, if a poet writes while both his parents are living? Of course. And yet, we as readers still crave to connect a poem to the poet's biography.

But in an age when oversharing personal information is ubiquitous to our culture, then what avenue of self-exploration can still feel daring, powerful, even just resonant? If all is revealed on Instagram, then what artistic purpose could a confessional mode provide? Or, to put it in another way, how does a lyric poet respond to this new situation? How can we touch on, or gesture toward, personal experience without descending into cheap diaristic navel-gazing?

One strategy that Damian Rogers uses in this poem, and one that I see a lot of elsewhere (including in my own work, I admit), is a coyness about how much of a dark truth is truly personal. We aren't sure how many of the experiences being referred to here are "confessions" and how many are just within the realm of the poet's imagination. And the blurriness of that line seems to be exactly the subject of the poem itself.

Starting with the second stanza, Rogers employs a war-weary older-sister tone that mixes flippant generalization ("We're all having a hard time," "some problems are . . .") with the implication that real darkness lurks beneath the surface. Nothing personal is yet revealed, but she nevertheless lands on a brilliant, biting discovery: "Some swear the pile is the only known / enemy of the hole." It's a new truism that could be applied to everything from road repair to sexual politics to drug abuse and it hovers over the rest of the poem like a guiding principle: a pile of words in a poem fighting the hole of meaninglessness, a small pile of cocaine fighting a feeling of emptiness in the addict, etc.

The speaker then turns her attention to address some "pretty girls tripping on night," and this is where the poem really takes off. Forgive me if, to my English professor ears, this phrase reminds me of T.S. Eliot's *The Waste Land* with its "O you who turn the wheel and look to windward, / Consider Phlebas, who was once handsome and tall as you." The failed Romanticism of the two passages, and the warning that contains elements of longing, feels similar.

But the source of disappointment in Rogers' poem is not quite so abstract or highfalutin as in Eliot's work. The images that follow are some of the various ways that young women put themselves at risk in search of a "pile" with which to combat their psychological "hole." Notice all the p's in the next sentence: "O pretty girls tripping on night, // enjoy this next round, as your pupils pour out / past last call." In a poem that hasn't yet called a lot of attention to its musicality, it's a notable moment of alliterative play, one that will recur later in the poem. But the music in use here is not a pretty one: multiple p sounds don't really sound "beautiful," but evoke something more like rough laughter or spitting.

Most of these "pretty girls" will likely survive their youthful misbehaviours "tripping on night" and the speaker seems to wish them well, but her interest zooms in on the one who will more dangerously lose her way: "One of you will stop caring // for your hair and your delicates will start to sour. / You will pick your teeth clean with your coke nail." I love how the prim euphemism

"delicates" contrasts with the more brutal and slangy "coke nail."
It's as if the speaker herself can't decide whose experience she
most relates to — the one who strays too far or the one who
observes her fall. The speaker's knowledge is intimate enough
that we wonder if she has been through it herself (how else would
she know?) but she refrains from saying so explicitly.

In the next stanza the camera lens pans back out to the group
of girls and the image of their primping is almost repulsive —
"lips slick with petroleum" — and she observes them leaving the
bar "down the black tube toward morning." The black tube could
refer to the lipstick tube from the previous line, a subway ride
home, or the more metaphoric tube/hole beckoning the young
women out to the future. Within that space is the flashiest sonic
music of the poem — "little pots of hot pink clink like crystal . . ."
— that evokes for me both desire and disgust in the speaker who
may look upon these younger women with something between
worry and yearning.

Her identification with the girls reaches its climax with the
accusatory (or is it just gossipy?) "Did you kiss the devil's ass / in
the alley?" But that question seems to trip a protective wire in the
speaker. She's gone far enough, she doesn't want to go farther,
and so she shuts down her line of thought with "Please, no more
questions." It's a wonderfully surprising line because of course
we *haven't* been asking any questions. Nevertheless the speaker
seems suddenly to feel our curiosity upon her, and she turns her-
self away. Weirdly it's that moment of refusal that reveals the
most vulnerability in the voice. We know that, in her opinion,
"We're all having a hard time," and so we can guess she has prob-
lems of her own, but until she puts her hand up, it doesn't occur
to us to wonder how deep those problems go.

In some ways this turning away exposes more than any explicit confession might. I remember an acting teacher once telling me that watching a performer struggle to hold back tears is often more moving to an audience than watching her cry onstage. It's our sense of the forces in conflict that connects us to a performance. Similarly, in "Ode to a Rolling Blackout" we feel the desire in Rogers' speaker to claim connection to the "pretty girls" and their adventures, but we also feel her desire to refrain from divulging the sources of her hard-won wisdom. Her reticence, her refusal to "dish," is as much what makes the speaker an adult as her ability to sidestep any ass-kissing in alleys.

This returns me to the question of authenticity. The speaker's position *between* confession and restraint, identification and distance, seems to me the central subject of the poem. And so whether or not the speaker of the poem, or the "real" Damian Rogers, knows what it's like to pick her teeth with her coke nail is less important than the feelings of trepidation, of empathy and worry, and even a bit of nostalgia for an earlier, more dangerous and exciting life that the poet reveals and explores. How much does she really know about it? The sufficient answer for the poem is "maybe some." And the more complete answer is "none of your damned business."

How a Poem Impersonates a Tomato

Oliver Bendorf, "Queer Facts about Vegetables"

My reading for the Griffin Prize introduced me to a number of young trans poets who are pioneering new ways of thinking about gender and identity in poetry. They are very different from each other, and so I don't want to make generalizations about what "trans poetry" might be, but I'm happy to be made newly aware of some emerging transgender poets who offer readers new challenges, questions, and realms of experience. One of these poets is Ali Blythe, whose poem "Shattered" we read a few pages back. Another is Oliver Bendorf, whose first collection, *The Spectral Wilderness*, won the Stan and Tom Wick Poetry Prize and was published by the Kent State University Press. Here's a poem from that collection:

Queer Facts about Vegetables

In 1893, the Supreme Court ruled unanimously that
the tomato is a vegetable.

I know I am a nightshade,
it says to its own limp vine.
I know how to burst

against teeth
with my juice and seed.
I'm as small

as a thumbnail, no,
I'm as big as the harvest
fucking sun.

I'm fresh blood
on a small curled fist.
I can be a boy, I know,

but never a man.
I can be Sunday gravy
or a pickled green.

This is still the tomato
talking to the vine,
as told to me.

— from *The Spectral Wilderness* (Kent State University Press, 2015)

This poem gets me right from the epigraph. As a footnote points out, taxation was one of the primary motivations the Supreme Court had for deliberately misclassifying tomatoes as vegetables in 1893. (If you're curious, you can find out more by looking up the Nix v. Hedden case.) The point is that classification is political, not just scientific or even practical. If this is true for fruits and vegetables, how much more so then is it for categories like "male" and "female"? In that context, it makes some sense that Bendorf would empathize with the subject of these legislative manoeuvres. But the antic gumption of speaking in the voice of the tomato is what delights me.

Bendorf sets out to explore the identity of a tomato, overheard speaking "to its own limp vine." Of course we know that it's the invisible poet orchestrating this, and (especially given the title, and other poems in the collection) we can be forgiven if we read the poem on the hunt for some sort of allegorical representation of what it is to be queer, trans, or simply trapped in overdetermined gender categories. Part of the fun Bendorf is having here is that he *knows* we're overreading the poem for insight into trans experience, and so he can toy with our trigger-happy metaphorizing impulses. He teases us with a line like "burst // against teeth / with my juice and seed," which perhaps we're tempted to read in a sexualized way but which seems to be, really, *just about the tomato.*

Meanwhile the tomato itself is not remotely interested in whether it is a fruit or a vegetable. Rather it declares itself to be a part of the nightshade family — a loosely defined scientific classification that includes a huge range of plants from chili peppers to eggplants to tobacco, and even to some toxic herbs like belladonna (deadly nightshade). Does the tomato claim membership in *this* arbitrarily defined identity group with any ambivalence? It doesn't seem so. So if some identifying categories fit more comfortably on us than others, the same seems true for the tomato.

The poem continues with the tomato recognizing some of its physical characteristics: it knows how it responds to being chewed, and understands (and exaggerates) its range of sizes, colors, and shapes. Tonally also the poem is feeling its way around, starting with a more formal proclamation ("I know I am a nightshade") and eventually breaking into the suddenly slangy-grandiose "I'm as big as the harvest / fucking sun." It's worth remembering that if this poem is about identity, the tomato is doing its best to answer our question. If someone were to ask, "Who are you?" how would any of us respond? We might very well assert these same sorts of family affiliations, physical characteristics, abilities, and desires.

But the poem makes a crucial slip between the fourth and fifth stanzas: "I can be a boy, I know, // but never a man." Could this really be the tomato speaking? In what way could a tomato be a boy but not a man? It appears as though for a moment the strain of the metaphoric construction has split, and that the poet himself has fallen out of the game and into confession. But if that's the case, then why can the *poetic speaker* only be a boy and not a man? How are we going to differentiate *these* two categories? What changes a boy into a man? Is it puberty, reproductive capability? Psychological maturity? Self-awareness? The poem doesn't offer clear answers, but it exposes an important question that complicates and deepens our understanding of the predicament of identity.

With the ending our poet recovers his composure, and shuts down the confession with an obvious lie: "This is still the tomato

How a Poem Seeks New Models

Shannon Maguire, "[The most visible ants are]"

I hope someone is working on a longer essay about Shannon Maguire's *Myrmurs* because I'm fascinated by the book and believe it deserves more in-depth attention than I can provide here. There are ambitious macro-structures at play (the book calls itself an "exploded sestina"), references to queer poetics and contemporary philosophy, and cool drawings of ants by David Bateman that I believe are meant to be in conversation with the poems. The book is unabashedly allusive and experimental, smart and playful. It invites an extended explanatory reading that could tease out the richness Maguire has implanted there. But I don't have the space for all that, so let me merely spend a bit of time with a nine-line poem that opens the collection to give a taste of its various trajectories and concerns. The poem, untitled, appears after the table of contents but before the epigraph and so is a sort of prologue or maybe even a kind of dedication:

The most visible ants are
(we venture into outer worlds) —
non-reproductive females

they build life-supporting
(we feed & protect each other) —
structures for their society

coordinate their work thru
(our pheromones &) —
body contact

— from *Myrmurs* (BookThug, 2015)

Two things strike me as a reader right away. First, the shape of the poem — with its regular short stanzas and repeated use of the long dash — summons Emily Dickinson for me. Even the rich, weirdly inventive metaphor of worker ants as a corollary for "non-reproductive females" and how they contribute to society seems to me something that Dickinson would get a kick out of. I'll go further into that metaphor momentarily.

The other thing that catches my eye is the back and forth between "we" and "they," which is underscored by the use of parentheses for all of the "we" statements. The parallel between the worker ants and "we" is very clear, but by holding back from unifying the pronouns Maguire stops short of implying that the two groups are the same. They are *connected* in the poem, but they are held *separate* by the grammar, line breaks, and punctuation. The limitations of the comparison are as important as the comparison itself.

So let's explore that parallel first, before pointing out some of its limitations. My perfunctory familiarity with ant sociobiology suggests to me that almost all of the important work in an ant colony gets done by workers and soldiers — both sterile females — and that only reproduction is handled by drones (reproductive males) and a single queen (reproductive female). Even the raising and feeding of larvae is handled by the workers. On the other hand, as I hope doesn't need to be pointed out, "non-reproductive females" have traditionally been marginalized (at best) by patriarchal societies including our own, leaving them without defined communal roles or value. By pointing out a highly organized social system like that of ants and emphasizing the crucial role that non-reproductive females play in it, Maguire simply and defiantly asserts that it doesn't have to be this way and that moreover it probably *already isn't* this way.

What's magical about the comparison Maguire sets up is that she doesn't need to explain any of this — the metaphor is never explicitly pointed out. There is no line in the poem that says, "Ain't we just like those ants?!" But the interweaving of the "we" statements in lines 2, 5, and 8 (which we might initially mistake as the voice of the worker ants themselves?) infers an affinity with "the most visible ants" referred to in the rest of the poem that encourages us to think further, to explore the implications. Who are the "we" in this poem? Which "non-reproductive females" are we talking about exactly? Do they really "build life-supporting . . . structures for their society"? Which structures are those? A full social critique opens up that provides numerous avenues for exploration in the rest of the book.

But let's be careful not to overstate the comparison. In the middle stanza, the ants of lines 1 and 3 may be constructing "life-supporting . . . structures for their society," but the speakers of the middle line "feed & protect each other." These are not exactly the same activities. In fact, given what we know about humanity, it seems likely that the "structures of their society" are precisely what human non-reproductive females women often need protection *from*. Or perhaps the structures they are building are *alternatives* to those already in existence? Either way, they are not exactly like the worker ants, whose social position is not up for debate. The human women who appear in the rest of *Myrmurs* will address these questions in greater detail, trying to decide which aspects of "normative" societal structures they find valuable, and which require revision, rebellion, or escape.

The last stanza brings the human and the ant back together somewhat. Here, the parentheses that have kept the human and the ant apart seem to blur — the sentence attempts to run over them. In other words, we can read the last stanza without the parenthesis and the sentence still coheres: both the ants and the women "coordinate their work thru . . . pheromones & . . . body contact." "Body contact" is a funny term here, one that could refer to a whole range of practices from (non-reproductive) sex to fistfighting to the types of chemical communication that ants seem to employ. This will be an important point of exploration for Maguire as well — that no matter how esoteric our thinking or abstract our ideas, we still inhabit physical bodies that have needs, discomforts, and desires, and that these cannot be held aloof from our intellectual or spiritual selves. The poem reminds us of the likelihood that the mind/body divide is itself a false binary invented by patriarchal Greek philosophy, and deserving of critique.

If it appears that I've explored how this poem moves partly as a way to point you to read the rest of *Myrmurs*, I'm fine with that. It's a short poem, but it opens up a lot of fascinating possibilities and serves as a very useful précis on what the rest of Maguire's excellent book attempts to achieve.

One last point. If you are not accustomed to reading so-called "experimental" poetry, "The most visible . . ." — and indeed most of *Myrmurs* — might seem decidedly "unpoetic." It isn't particularly musical in its approach to language, it eschews regular meter, and it doesn't really paint vivid images in the mind. A poem like this isn't trying to do what, say, Raoul Fernandes' "Life with Tigers," does in its evocation of scene or mood. What it *is* trying to do is provoke the intellectual imagination. Its rhyme is implication, its metrics are social critique. Shannon Maguire does make more lyric gestures elsewhere in *Myrmurs*, but I think it's all right to accept that her primary strength here is associative rather than imagistic. If that makes it a new kind of poem for your experience, good. Be not afeard. To belabour the metaphor of this book's title, this poem doesn't "move" the way Raoul Fernandes' poem moves, or the way a poem by Keats or Elizabeth Bishop or Oliver Bendorf moves. But it does move — with energy, smarts, and its own kind of grace.

How a Poem Makes Itself Out of Unusual Materials

Madhur Anand, "Especially in a Time"

Poetry has always used other texts to do more with its small space: biblical allusions, or quotations from pop song lyrics, have been common in poetry for a long time, because they allow a poet to conjure or connote more than a stand-alone image or phrase. But recent years have brought about an explosion of poems wrought exclusively from other texts: centos, which are formed by shuffling together lines from other poems and/or lyrics; erasures, which pick a text and erase selected parts to reveal other messages; and other kinds of mashups, remixes, and found poems. The connection to contemporary musical production seems worth emphasizing — like hip-hop sampling, these kinds of poetic techniques demonstrate a different kind of virtuosity, more akin to an archaeologist's or a collagist's than a traditional image-maker's, though you still have to be able to spot a great image or phrase in order to make it work in a poem. If Michelangelo said something about uncovering the angel in a block of stone, then some poets are able to see an aardvark in the angel.

One question that hovers over poems like this is: how does the new incarnation reflect back, enrich, challenge, or renew its source text? I could probably scour the text of *Moby-Dick* in order to create a shopping list for my weekend ("a draught of a draught . . . of wet . . . whiteness . . ."), but that wouldn't make it a worthwhile poem. What does the new poem *do* with its materials?

Madhur Anand has a Ph.D. in theoretical ecology, and her book *A New Index for Predicting Catastrophes* is at home in the language of science — its vocabulary, subjects, and syntactical patterns. "Especially in a Time" is one of a number of poems from the collection that are, as she explains it, "composed solely from words and phrases found" in scientific articles she has co-published. These poems, then, are a kind of remix of biological research. In the case here the paper is called "Rapid morphological change in stream beetle museum specimens correlates with climate change," by Jennifer Babin-Fenske, Madhur Anand, and Yves Alarie, which was published in the journal *Ecological Entomology* in 2008. Here's the poem:

Especially in a Time

Wild populations recognize that the linearity,
the relative rareness, the major museums, or any area
which is known, is a surrogate
for proximity

Stream beetles, Galapagos finches, and Israeli
passerine birds are transformed
into an index of limited
available information

Elytral lengths, slope of the regression,
and mid-latitude precipitation
unravel the anomalies

A prolonged change is also under scrutiny
— from *A New Index for Predicting Catastrophes*
(McClelland & Stewart, 2015)

I read through the study that is being mined here (Anand graciously provided a copy for me), and what struck me about the paper is how careful and tentative it is. Because it wants to be certain about what it is claiming, the essay is full of qualifications, admissions of speculation and incomplete data, and conjectures about mediating or conflicting factors. This may be a common trope in scientific literature — I admit I don't read a lot of research papers in ecology — but in Anand's poem that doubtful precision emerges centre stage.

The poem takes a hold of this idea in the very first stanza: "Wild populations recognize that . . . " a bunch of things " . . .

is a surrogate / for proximity." This is a sneaky way to unfold scientific language in order to indict the very sort of scientific project described in the paper. In other words, all of the ways we non-wild populations have to study the world, all of the practices at the disposal of science — isolating anomalies ("relative rareness"), coherent argument ("linearity"), broad comparative systems ("major museums") — all of these techniques are merely substitutes for the knowledge by "proximity" that the "wild populations" have.

The second stanza continues on this track, noting that the collections of sample data from various species are really just "an index of limited / available information." It's worth pointing out that Anand has picked some delightful examples to illustrate this point. There's the near-rhyme between "stream" and "passerine," and the quick tour around the world from the focus of her research to the ends of the Earth and back to one of the centres of the ancient world. These choices bear Anand's poetic fingerprints most tellingly, because after having perused the source article, I note her choice of "Israeli passerine" over other equally illustrative examples from the text like "gastropod size" or "introduced toad species."

This points to another aspect of poems that draw from other texts — as much as forms of archeology, they are also acts of *curation*, and in that sense they are closer in technique to "regular" poems than they might seem. "Surrogate" and "proximity" are a full paragraph away from each other in Anand's source text, and so it is Anand the poet who has put them together. In a way every poet draws from a similar (if larger) lexicon of possible terms and phrases when she writes a poem, and so the constraint of drawing from a five-page scientific essay is not so very different than the constraint of, say, forcing each line to fit into a thirteen-syllable structure or the demands of a rhyming sonnet.

I'm trying to make a point here about how certain recent "experimental" techniques strike me as being very similar in practice to other kinds of constraints in poetry like the use of rhyme, or meter, or syllabic count, or whatever. Self-important poets *and* intimidated readers often see these practices as a radical departure from previous forms of poetry, but for me, "use only words that appear in this essay" is a kissing cousin to the directive, "use only words that rhyme with Innisfree." This doesn't diminish the delight at all — on the contrary, the virtuosity required to pull off the conceit *enhances* our delight, or at least it's meant to.

Anyway, it seems to me that in "Especially in a Time," Anand's skills as a source-mining poet highlight the tension between the search for truth and the barriers to discovering it. I want to be careful though about superimposing too much artificial "meaning" into some of the choices she makes, because part of the fun of a mashup like this is relishing the juxtapositions of scientific and quasi-poetic terminologies that don't quite cohere. As the poem closes, Anand seems drawn to phrases like "elytral lengths" (referring to the hardened wing-cases found on many beetles), equally for their sonic richness as for their relevance for studying the effects of climate change on micro-populations. But we seem to be a long way from unravelling all the anomalies.

In the end we are left with "a prolonged change" that is "also under scrutiny." It seems like a euphemism for powerlessness — "under scrutiny" speaks to scientific and literary attention, but also to a kind of bureaucratic societal paralysis in the face of tremendous, and terrifying, global trends. Our successes are incremental, incomplete, and qualified, and yet the search for scientific truth and poetic beauty continue. Should we despair because of our inability to discover the kind of sky-opening revelations that will propel the world to change? Or do we keep collecting specimens?

How a Poem Chooses the
Apocalypse Behind Curtain #3

Jennifer L. Knox, "The New Let's Make a Deal"

The connection between comedy and tragedy, or between laughter and darkness, is well documented. The trick, in poetry as in any other art form, is the balancing act — if there's too much fun and silliness, then any attempt to add gravity feels false or awkward. If there's too much tragedy, then the jokes fall flat.

Jennifer L. Knox has made a career out of high-wiring the balance between raucous comedy and searing tragedy. Here's a poem from her book *Days of Shame & Failure*:

The New *Let's Make a Deal*

The bedazzled tribe of yahoos has returned
with a new too-tanned, top-heavy prize bunny
swishing her porny French manicure 'round a Frigidaire.
Monty's boorish plaid: swapped for Wayne Brady,
dapper in gray. A woman dressed like a bumblebee,
penciled brows arched in permashock, weighs her options:
a bright pink bow-tied box, or the unknown thing
behind curtain #3. She squints into the din of hoots,
wrings her hands. Life could be made easy in an instant.
"I pick the curtain." Attagirl. The box was a gag: a ham
with straps attached to it. A ham bag. Get it?
Wayne takes a bite to prove the meat's really real
and the audience goes totes bonkers . . . we're interrupted
by news of the hurricane. U.N. delegates have gone on
hunger strike until "a meaningful outcome" is reached.
God, give us one hundred more years until the dawn
of the Kingdom of Roaches, until the sea reclaims Death Valley,
until the end. *Hey, what kind of poem is this?* Behind curtain #3:
a combo washer-dryer bright as a mirrored iceberg.
Bee lady does a shrieking pogo while a guy in a dinosaur
costume mouths, "I love you, Mom!" into the camera.
It's that kind of poem: a poem for the end of the world.
— from *Days of Shame & Failure* (Bloof Books, 2015)

Now, it's probably true that *every* poem about a game show
is actually a poem about the apocalypse. But before we get to the
bottom of things, let's take a bit of time to admire how much
Knox packs into those opening lines. The language is rich,

dense, and hilarious. I want to suggest that there's something about the rampant use of trochees that adds to the tumbling, brutal absurdity of it all. (Trochees are the opposite of iambs, they go DUM-dum DUM-dum, like a heartbeat.) So "BUNny / SWISHing her PORNy . . ." or "MONty's BOORish PLAID." Like a good standup comedian, Knox has chosen her language very carefully, to pack the biggest punch, and it's only when we look again that we see how well-crafted it is. I'm not going to, but trust me when I say I could write a full paragraph on the brilliance that is "She squints into the din of hoots."

There's also an element of scorn that I want to highlight, because despite its wit, the attitude our speaker takes with the "yahoos" on TV isn't something we are meant to feel 100 percent comfortable with. It's easy enough to make fun of the contestants on shows like *Let's Make a Deal*, especially their cartoonish enthusiasms. But we also know that they're being cast and coached to "go big" for our entertainment. And as the poem progresses, our own role as active audience members is increasingly implicated. And so while the speaker of the poem is mocking them with gleeful precision, there's a cruelty here that's going to turn on itself momentarily.

Meanwhile, as we pass by, stick a pin in "Life could be made easy in an instant." This desire for simplicity, for an easy life, is also something I want to put pressure on.

The poem makes a big turn at the end of line 13 — from "totes bonkers" to news of a hurricane. A storm big enough for the NBC affiliate to interrupt its daytime programming. And our speaker calls it "*the*" hurricane, as if she already knows about it, as if this isn't the first update she's heard. From the hurricane we travel to more bad news about U.N. delegates on a hunger strike. As far as I know, the only actual example of a U.N. delegate launching a hunger strike is when Naderev Sano, from the Philippines, did so in 2013 to urge the U.N. to take stronger action on climate change. This was in the aftermath of Typhoon Haiyan, the deadliest on record in the Philippines, which killed over six thousand people in that country alone.

Knox isn't necessarily referring directly to these particular events, but the point is that there are serious, even cataclysmic, things going on in the world. Meanwhile, we're watching *Let's Make a Deal*. The lines that follow indicate that our speaker realizes how desperate the situation is, but her prayer for "one hundred more years" isn't really a solution. In fact it's a tremendously selfish desire — don't solve the problem, God, just give us one hundred more years, after which I'll be dead anyhow. Is praying for a solution to *climate change* beyond the imagination of this speaker? I mean, as long as we're *praying . . .* ! Why are her desires merely for a stay of execution rather than a Presidential pardon?

For a moment, then, as a reader I am prepared to turn against the speaker of this poem, and to judge her as just as superficial as the game show contestants she's been mocking. But then Knox turns the tables on me once again: "*Hey, what kind of poem is this?*" That's *my* voice asking this question. Knox catches us just before we are tempted to leave the room. Whether it's because of my ethical doubts or because we want to finally, *finally*, learn what's behind curtain #3, our impatience finds voice inside the poem, and the poem returns us to what's most important.

Tell the truth, when you were reading, you were a little glad that the poem turned back to curtain #3 and that Bee Lady won her washer-dryer, weren't you? You weren't hoping for more lines about Typhoon Haiyan, or any other terrible storm, or hunger strikes or climate change or the U.N. Whatever well-meaning actions you as an individual reading this essay have performed today to avert climate change, it is most definitely not enough to solve the problem. Whatever you can do, it's not enough. You are powerless before the forces — meteorological, economic, historical — that doom us to destruction. And so no wonder we long for our easy entertainments, including the entertainment of making fun of those who give us those easy answers. The world is careening toward destruction, but Bee Lady has a new (energy efficient? water conserving?) washer-dryer to make her life easier and good.

This is partly why this poem really *is* about the end of the world, as it admits in the final line. The poem has pivoted from the game show and the disasters to the subject ultimately being about our childish, understandable response to our powerlessness. That's the real tragedy underneath the comedy.

These daring leaps are what separates Knox's poem from other poets, whether they are climate activists or pop culture satirists. The fact that she can get all that into one poem, as well as our wavering between moral horror and simple glee, is totes bonkers.

How a Poem Assembles a Smashed Record for Posterity

George Murray, from "#DaydreamBereaver"

List poems are fun. They're fun to write, and they're often fun to read. The poet has no obligation to follow a line of thought, or description, and so list poems lend themselves to freewheeling non-sequitur, to invention, to play. And yet, no matter how weird, disparate, or far-ranging a list is, we cannot help but try to sculpt it into some kind of coherence. It's the curse of being good readers: we are *trained* to find connections, and so, even if there are none, we find them.

Of course a good poet is aware of all this and uses our expectations to her advantage. The late C.D. Wright's terrific list poem "Personals," for example, leaves enough of a trail for us to put together a portrait of a scene, a character, and a situation. The artist Jenny Holzer uses the form and language of slogans to create list poems in space that, among other things, parody corporate advertising.

As soon as I started working on this project I knew that I wanted to write about George Murray's *Diversion*, but I've had a problem because most of the poems are well over thirty lines long. For the sake of keeping my essays readably short, I've needed to stick with shorter pieces. And so finally I asked Murray's permission to use just a section from one of the poems — you won't get the full picture here, but I hope you can get a sense of what he's after and that it will encourage you to dive more deeply into this funny, inventive, often disturbing collection.

Diversion is a whole book of list poems with titles like "#CivilDisconvenience" and "#SocialMedea." The ubiquitous hashtag mark points us to the quick wit and quick rancour we tend to find online, the unpredictable mashup of the profane and the profound. In these two titles you can also see one of his recurring techniques — twisting familiar phrases into new creations. Here are the last ten lines from a poem called "#DaydreamBereaver":

> Homecoming queen becomes homestaying queen.
> Disciples follow the guide with the umbrella and
>   megaphone.
> One flew over the cuckoo's nest but the rest of us
>   landed in it.
> Death switched to a pistol after complaints a scythe
>   wasn't individual-enough attention.
> I like big buts and I cannot lie.

Freedom is the space found after the last channel on
    the dial.

The sound of our culture is the sound of a fat ass flopping
    onto a toilet seat.

12 reasons you need to try this before you die! are 11
    more than needed to convince me.

What you're reading is a black box.

Bet you a dozen beers the first intelligent thought was
    a wish.

    — from *Diversion* (ECW Press, 2015)

One challenge with list poems is how to keep them interesting — if there's no story, description, or argument to pull us through to the end, the poet has to work extremely hard to vary the form, tone, and materials in order to keep the reader engaged, even off-balance. The poet must land punches from different directions. So notice first how Murray varies the syntax, the tone, even the pronouns in these ten lines. First person pronouns are used four times, second person in the last three. Two lines make sweeping generalizations (about disciples and freedom). Two lines report mini-narratives: about homecoming queens whose lives lose their sparkle and a cartoonish Death who can be influenced by popular opinion. Lines that start off like serious statements become jokes, and vice versa (especially the last line).

Murray's most scatological images tend to disguise a more complicated point. While we may grimace at "the sound of a fat ass flapping onto a toilet seat," we are compelled to confront a more ambitious, if somewhat facetious, comment about what sounds "our culture" actually makes. Even better is his repurposing of an early '90s rap masterpiece (Sir Mix-a-Lot's "Baby Got Back," which brought us the unforgettable lyric, "I like big butts and I cannot lie"). It's worth mentioning that "Baby Got Back" is ultimately a song about rejecting false-perfection and fakery in pop culture portrayals of feminine beauty. Murray uses the lyric punningly to point to a core concept in *Diversion*: that reversals, "buts," are an antidote to lazy and complacent thinking.

As we reel from Murray's inventiveness and fun we also start to sense a recurring frustration with contemporary culture, even in the glib wordplay that the poems themselves utilize. Murray's self-deprecation about how he's a sucker for internet clickbait like "reasons to try this before you die!" churns along with "the rest of us land[ing]" in the cuckoo's nest. If disciples just follow whoever has an umbrella and megaphone, and the way to freedom is just past our ever-expanding channel selection, then our culture really will increasingly sound as unpleasant and grotesque as a fat ass on a toilet seat. The lines, which seemed so separate and chaotic at first glance, begin to speak to each other.

For me, this culminates in the quietly devastating line, "What you're reading is a black box." An airplane's black box is only important to most of us if the plane crashes, as a record of what happened, so that we might discover what went wrong. So too this poem and this collection. *Diversion* makes claims about itself as a sort of recording device that, with logorrhoeic glee, simultaneously mocks, preserves, and celebrates our contemporary moment. It might be tempting to dismiss it as a prodigious, bawdy gathering of witticisms or reworked detritus of popular culture and internet meme-making, but the poems also serve as a record of a societal vessel that is careening toward destruction. Perhaps those who come to clean up the aftermath will be able to deduce something from this wreckage. It's not a comforting thought, but it adds a layer of seriousness and challenge to the fun.

How a Poem Tries to Connect Us, Despite the Obstacles

Donna Stonecipher's "Model City [4]"

Model City [4]

It was like seeing a fox one day right in the middle of the city —
a real fox, not a taxidermied fox, nor a fox logo, nor a foxy person
that one might want to sleep with.

*

It was like stopping and staring at the fox, along with all the
other people walking down the street, all stopped in their
tracks and staring in astonishment at the fox.

*

It was like watching the real, soft, cinnamon-colored fox, the only object moving in the landscape, moving silkily along the overgrown median, darting glances over at the people standing on the sidewalk, staring.

*

It was like the concentrated attention placed on the fox's perplexing appearance deflected by the fox, who keeps moving down the street, headed to a fox den known only to the fox — dark, liquid, solvent.

— from *Model City* (Shearsman Books, 2015)

Donna Stonecipher's *Model City* is a strange and wonderful book, with seventy-two poems that all look like the one above: four prose sections/stanzas/paragraphs, each beginning with "It was like . . . " At first they seem to be about inhabiting a "model city," or "garden city" as they're sometimes called, trying to explore the sensations one might have in the midst of planned architecture and street design. The utopian vision that is behind any model city — "if we plan this correctly everyone will be happy" — lends itself to all sorts of artificial weirdness, and so we can see how being *inside* those ideas might be ripe for poetic exploration.

But as the poems accumulate, it gets harder and harder to figure out what the "it" in "it was like" is really referring to. In his blurb for the book, Noah Eli Gordon calls it a "missing antecedent," and in many of the poems the opening phrase seems less like an answer to the question, "What was travelling through the model city like?" and more like an answer to the question, "What was it like to be a human being in the early twenty-first century?" The answers the poems provide are not exactly logical, but they are still somehow clarifying.

Which is why the "It was like . . . " form works so well for me. Like a stutter, or a grasping at ideas, the speaker of these poems always seems on the verge of discovering what "it" was like, but can't satisfy herself that she's found the best simile for her mix of thoughts and feelings. In this way the poem, indeed the whole book, seems like an exploration, a series of attempts to reach out to us, her readers, to try to bridge the inevitable gap between one individual experience and another.

In this particular poem, these attempts all revolve around the appearance of a fox in a cityscape. It's worth remembering that in a perfect "model city," we probably wouldn't see a real fox at all on any "overgrown meridian." But in the first section what's even stranger is that the speaker has to clarify what kind of fox we're seeing: "not a taxidermied fox, nor a fox logo, nor a foxy person that one might want to sleep with." Are we really likely to confuse these things with each other? If we were there on the street, the clarification would be ridiculous. The only place where we might get confused is in a poem. It's the first hint we have of Stonecipher's efforts to travel through the page to us, against the limits of language and misunderstanding. The poem wants to be very careful in order to communicate, to make sure we understand what "it was like."

The second stanza focuses on how the speaker feels connected to everyone around her who is similarly awestruck at the appearance of the animal. She goes from "stopping and staring" to noticing that everyone around her is also "stopped . . . and staring." Even the artless repetition of the verbs seems a reflection of her dumbfounded-ness ("staring" will get used once more, in the following section). I find myself wondering if the speaker's need to feel communal connection is partly a result of her being in a model city. I'm no expert, but I sense that artificial constructions like model cities suppress organic, roughened, unpredictable experiences, and so the shared communal staring is a minor breakthrough that the speaker longs for in the same way she longs to break through the page to us.

The fox is now the "only object moving in the landscape," and in the poem. Notice that "it" is never actually compared to the fox itself — it was like *seeing* the fox, *stopping and staring* at the fox, *watching* the fox, and the *attention placed* on the fox. The poem, and the comparison — what "it" was like — is really about our experience of encountering the fox, together. "The attention placed" is singular, even though it's a crowd of people who are focusing their various attentions on the creature, and that crowd now includes us too, who have spent four stanzas seeing, stopping and staring, watching, and placing our attention there.

Meanwhile the actual fox is beyond our efforts to associate with it. Our attention is "deflected" while it carries on with its business, eventually disappearing into its invisible home in the midst of our urban, urbane constructions — our city, our streets, and our poems. I love the last word here, "solvent," which literally means "able to dissolve other substances." At the beginning of the poem, the fox's appearance (and Stonecipher's poem about it) dissolves our individuality into a collective sense of awe. But at the end of the poem, the den, by removing the object of our attention from the scene, dissolves our shared experience, dissolves the scene and the poem. We are returned to our singular selves.

How a Poem Welcomes Us
to the Neighbourhood

Bren Simmers, "[Night of nesting dolls]"

How do you evoke a sense of place in a poem? How does a poem communicate what it feels like to be somewhere, not just as a tourist, but as a local, an inhabitant, someone who belongs? This seems especially tricky in an urban landscape. How do you trace *belonging* in a space that is poor in the flora and fauna that usually bring magic to a poem of place?

Bren Simmers' second book, *Hastings-Sunrise* (Nightwood Editions, 2015), makes its home in the Vancouver neighbourhood of its title, and unapologetically, even possessively, *inhabits* that neighbourhood. My friend Paul tells me that Vancouver writers have a special knack for evoking their neighbourhoods in poetry and fiction, and I will defer to his wider reading on the subject. So maybe it's something about Vancouver? I can't say, but there's a dissertation in there somewhere for somebody.

Most of Simmers' poems in this collection are untitled, and are organized around the time of year, so we trace the area of Hastings-Sunrise over the course of a seasonal cycle. She starts with a table of contents that is actually a rough map of the "21 x 13 blocks" of her neighbourhood, and adds playful charts of valuable local information such as "Map of Neighborhood Swings," "Map of Open Doors," lists of businesses opened and closed, "Map of Christmas Lights," etc. Cumulatively, over the course of the book, we start to feel at home in some of the recurring cross-streets and sightlines, but before we get to that point, here's one poem from the first section of the book, which takes place during spring:

Night of nesting dolls,
many layers held
inside this one:
cocktails on the balcony,
supper at eight, the after-
dinner doubles games,
while kids pump legs
on swing sets.
At sundown, an old man
shuffles three times
around the park. Nightly,
I've started to look for
his cross-country gait,
tan paperboy cap,

started to call him *ours*.
Then falls the deep blue
scrim and the few
stars we can spot
amid shipyard cranes
and lights on Grouse.
So brief,
the smallest doll
is sleep.

— from *Hastings-Sunrise* (Nightwood Editions, 2015)

There's some lovely music and image-making here, but I want to spend most of my space unpacking the way Simmers organizes this poem, via the overarching image of nesting dolls. I find something delightfully odd in the progression and believe it reveals some real insight into how we encounter our little near-dwellings (neigh/nigh = near, bur = dwelling), our neighbourhoods, and ultimately ourselves.

If I were to tell you that I was going to write a poem describing a landscape using nesting dolls as a metaphor, you'd probably assume that I would use the first, largest nesting doll to represent the world, the sky, the wider topography, elevation and longitude and such things. Subsequent "dolls" would narrow the focus in space until the smallest dolls might represent my street, my house, my living room, my couch, etc. Organizing the poem spatially would make a certain logical sense, but it would also be pretty predictable and boring.

It would also, ultimately, be a dumb way to explore how we *connect* to our landscape. On a day-to-day basis, we don't relate to our neighbourhoods thinking about elevation and longitude, but rather through the lens of our own lives, what we're doing in the landscape, how we are living in it. So Simmers scatters the spatial, and starts with "cocktails on the balcony, / supper at eight" etc. The largest nesting doll, the one that contains everything else in the poem, is the set of actions that the speaker is performing on what seems like a pleasant, leisurely spring evening near a park.

We might also read the largest frame for the poem as being one of mood or tone, setting us up as readers to view the world here through a lens of ease and affection. Subsequent poems might reframe our encounter with Hastings-Sunrise through gloom or anger or worry or frustration (as indeed some do), but for now, for tonight, at the opening of this poem, we get to see the area at its most welcoming.

Once we know what we're doing, and how we're feeling, we can start to see the world around us, and the next nesting doll contains a living neighbour, "an old man" who daily "shuffles three times / around the park." Our speaker knows him well enough to expect him every night, to recognize his "tan paperboy cap" (notice the nice assonance of the flat *a*'s there), to know how many times he circles the park, even to weirdly think of him as "ours," but not well enough to know his name, or where he's arriving from. It's worth pointing out that even here, during the course of the poem, our speaker sidesteps the opportunity to introduce herself to her old man, so there are clearly limits to the spirit of community that she feels, even under the ideal circumstances of this poem. Why not take a break from playing doubles to say hello? In another poem from the book, the speaker feels a tinge of jealousy when, at a coffee shop, the barista calls out to another customer by name, but the tinge isn't enough for her to go ahead and make herself known. Something of urban personal boundaries, or a desire for privacy, or just plain-old Canadian embarrassment, remains, which also speaks to the kind of life our speaker has in Hastings-Sunrise — a life whose connection to those around her is not absolute, or fully without mistrust. There are good reasons for this, and they appear in other poems from the book, but here, given the lighter mood, it's just a lingering reticence.

Meanwhile, if we are back and forth in space, we are fairly consistent in time, moving through the evening, cocktails on the balcony, after-dinner activities in the park, and ultimately, inevitably, darkness falling and night coming on.

Oddly, as night falls, the description of the landscape is at its most specific. The shipyard cranes make this a fairly unusual cityscape, and I assume "Grouse" refers to Grouse Mountain, the well-known Vancouver landmark that can be seen quite clearly from the parts of Hastings-Sunrise that approach the water. Again, notice the reticence though — our speaker is willing to locate herself close enough to the harbour to see the cranes and the lights on Grouse, but she won't tell us which street she lives on herself. Even to us, her readers, there's a slight holding back.

(Can I say as an aside that I believe the word "grouse" to be one of the ugliest words in the English language? I mean that in a good way.)

The blessing and curse of belonging to a place, any place, is that it shrinks our horizons; if you belong somewhere, especially in an urban environment, you're only going to see a narrow slice of sky. And so as the poem starts to close down, Simmers gestures toward the limitations of planting herself in Hastings-Sunrise knowing that doing so very literally narrows her vision of the rest of the world.

The final image, "the smallest doll / is sleep," evokes the satisfaction we feel at the end of a good day, shutting down our outward-gazing selves and hunkering down into our smallest spaces, the spaces that are most our own. But it also gives voice to complaint ("so brief") and to the limitations of our individual selves, trapped in the narrowness of the world inside our eyelids. We might dream of a wider world, but we can't build a home there.

I admire this poem, and indeed the whole collection *Hastings-Sunrise*, because it accepts the richness *and* limitations of being home in a neighbourhood, but also being at home in an individual self who (in most cases) must choose just one place in which to make her life.

How a Poem Evokes Wonder

Sarah Holland-Batt, "Botany"

Sarah Holland-Batt is an Australian poet who has spent considerable time in the United States. If I had the gumption I might try to make claims about how her work straddles the poetic traditions of both nations, but it seems a bit premature since the poem below is from only her second book, *The Hazards*, and so I hope we'll be hearing a lot more from her before these kinds of evaluations become worthwhile. One thing I will say is that she, like many other Australian poets I've read, derives real delight from the natural world of her homeland, a world which often seems to me to be more beautiful, dangerous, and bizarre than my own.

Botany

After the rain, we went out in pairs
to hunt the caps that budded at night:
wet handfuls of waxtips and widows,
lawyer's wigs, a double-ringed yellow.

We shook them out onto gridded sheets,
the girls more careful than the boys,
pencilled notes on their size and shape,
then levelled a wood-press over their heads.

Overnight, they dropped scatter patterns
in dot-and-dash, spindles and asterisks
that stained the page with smoky rings,
blush and blot, coal-dust blooms.

In that slow black snow of spores
I saw a woodcut winter cart and horse
careen off course, the dull crash
of iron and ash, wheels unraveling.

All day, a smell of loam hung overhead.
We bent like clairvoyants at our desks
trying to divine the message left
in all those little deaths, the dark, childless stars.

        — from *The Hazards* (University of Queensland Press, 2015)

How do we translate wonder onto the page? We all experience awe from time to time when we encounter amazing things in the natural world — a spectacular sunset, a bear rummaging in a wood, a tornado — but writing about those encounters rarely summons corresponding feelings in the reader. In fact I think it's fair to say that, after the love poem, the "nature poem" is the type most frequently done badly. Not just because it's such well-trodden ground, but also because, like love, awe is a very difficult feeling to evoke or describe.

"Botany" tackles this problem in two ways. Firstly Sarah Holland-Batt has a wonderful ear, and her alliterative play, near rhymes, and metrical savvy combine to give this poem real brightness and sparkle. The beginning of the third stanza is particularly rich: "dropped scatter patterns / in dot-and-dash, spindles and asterisks" just feels fun in my mouth as I say it, the percussive *s*'s, *p*'s, *k*'s, and *t*'s bouncing off each other. And so even though the natural phenomena that she is describing — mushrooms — don't make a lot of noise (to my knowledge!), "Botany" translates some of their uniqueness into linguistic beauty, which we experience as sound.

One quick note about meter. This poem gestures toward a regular rhythmic pattern but never settles into it consistently. Many of the lines at the beginning are in a loose iambic tetrameter (four beats per line) and a few fit it perfectly: line 6, for example ("the GIRLS more CAREful THAN the BOYS"), as well as lines 11 and 13. For me, when a poet flirts with regular meter like this, it gives a kind of pulse to the poem, but one that is open to movement and flow. It provides a steady walking pace that can accommodate the occasional stumble or brief sprint. It's worth noting, then, that as the poet's fascination increases at the end, the poem adds another foot to the meter, so that in the last stanza we're mostly five beats to the line and the final line has six beats. It's as if, when the children's attention draws closer to the spore patterns, the speaker of the poem needs to cram more stress into each line to make room for her fascination.

Can we also, by the way, thank the botanist who originally named a species of mushroom "lawyer's wig"? Can that person please be honoured in some public fashion?

The other way that Holland-Batt evokes our wonder is by not limiting herself to the children's perspective, despite the school-time focus of the action. The evocative species names, the brief gesture toward gender politics ("the girls more careful than the boys"), the magic of the mushrooms' reaction under the wood-press — all of these are phenomena that most children would appreciate and understand. But something different happens in the fourth stanza. The mushrooms have made various spore patterns on the paper the students have spread under them, and the speaker starts to see images in the shapes that have been cre-ated by the "slow black snow of spores" (another wonderful lyric line). In her memory, the speaker sees something wild and hor-rific in the spore dust: a crashing horse-and-cart. Is this really the imagination of a child looking at the patterns, or an adult drawing pictures in her memory? Perhaps the girl had just read *Black Beauty*? But it feels more like we are progressing from the experience of the school children to the more mature wonder of the image-making adult.

Similarly, and more definitively, in the final stanza, the kids become "clairvoyants" (even the word would likely be inacces-sible to most school children) who are attempting to interpret the signs left by the mushrooms. And the poet brings to our attention the fact that the spores, because they have been deposited on paper instead of earth, won't be able to germinate and are therefore a display of "little deaths" for the individual mushrooms that have been harvested. Now I don't think the speaker of the poem is trying to evoke *regret* in us for the demise of these fine fungal specimens. On the contrary, it seems to me that the fragility, the strangeness, and the resilience of Earth's life forms (from dust . . .) is what transforms the children's awe into something that we adults might share. By leaving us with that weird bit of darkness, drummed home with the haunting final adjective "childless," this poem opens up a layer that is beyond the reach of the students in the poem, but which is palpable to those of us who read it.

How a Poem Reaches for Transcendence

Eric Pankey, "Ash"

Religious poetry was probably the first kind of poetry, but that
doesn't make it easy to write. What impresses me about this
poem is how it is unafraid to draw from various traditions and
approaches in a small space, while confronting a religious diffi-
culty that is both ancient and very contemporary.

Ash

At the threshold of the divine, how to know
But indirectly, to hear the static as
Pattern, to hear the rough-edged white noise as song —

Wait, not as song — but to intuit the songbird
Within the thorn thicket, safe, hidden there.
Every moment is not a time for song

or singing. Imagine a Buddha, handmade,
Four meters high of compacted ash, the ash
Remnants of joss sticks that incarnated prayer.

With each breath, the whole slowly disintegrates.
With each footfall, ash shifts. The Buddha crumbles.
To face it, we efface it with our presence.

An infant will often turn away as if
Not to see is the same as *not being seen.*
There was fire, but God was not the fire.

           — from *Crow-Work* (Milkweed Editions, 2015)

We start "on the threshold of the divine" — that is, *near*
something mysterious, revelatory, but not in it or on it or whatever. The first sentence of the poem is abstract, and at first the
poet might seem to be wondering about how to get over that
threshold, but that's not it. Instead he wants to learn "how to
know / But indirectly." In a sense the desire he's articulating
is about living comfortably *on* the threshold, to have his ear
pricked to what's happening over it. As Pankey zeroes in on this
idea he's able to find metaphors to approach it — the static, and
then the songbird. There are problems in both though: hearing
"the static as pattern," for example, would be an illusion, finding
meaning or intention in a phenomenon that actually has none.
(An atheist's accusation of the foolishness of a believer is that

she sees a pattern in static.) On the other hand, Pankey's form of belief isn't quite ready to proclaim an actual bird singing in the thicket ("Wait — not as song"), but only the possibility of *intuiting* a hidden presence there. Pankey's language is exploratory, tentative, careful — there are so many obstacles to portraying genuine religious experience, and he seems to be trying to navigate between the obvious pitfalls.

One of those pitfalls is simply focusing attention on a sensation that is supposed to function outside of articulate thought. By writing the poem at all, Pankey gestures toward feelings that defy or transcend language, and so his next step — the most vivid image of the poem and the one that takes up the most space here — is about how our very conscious presence precludes the possibility of pure revelation.

The image of the crumbling ash Buddha evokes a few things for me. First, Pankey is referring specifically to the work of artist Zhang Huan, who constructed a sculpture called *Ash Buddha*, which was literally a large Buddha made out of ash, at the Sidney Festival in early 2015, and has done similar work elsewhere. (You can find some wonderful depictions of his work online.) One essential aspect of the work is that it disintegrates over time, partly because of the presence of the people who view it. Another is that the ash itself is gathered from the remnants of others' religious rituals ("Remnants of joss sticks that incarnated prayer"), and so represents a kind of accumulation of faithful gestures.

The image of the disintegrating Buddha also seems connected to the "observer effect," an idea in quantum mechanics that certain phenomena are disturbed by any attempt to measure them. The familiar illustrative example is tire pressure: in order to measure tire pressure, you have to let a bit of air out of the tire, which slightly changes the very pressure you're trying to measure. Contrary to our usual scientific practice, observation in these cases is an obstacle to understanding.

A similar notion has been present in poetry since the Romantics — the idea that we can't *describe* transcendent feelings (religious, emotional, artistic, sexual, etc.) and *experience* them at the same time. For Keats, in "Ode to a Nightingale," the choice is to fall from the ecstasy of hearing the nightingale song in order to write his poem or, by submitting to it permanently, "become a sod."

For Pankey the choice is to face the ash Buddha and accept that our presence will contribute to its disintegration, or to turn away and take it on trust that the Buddha still stands. It's worth noting that the first word of this description (starting on line 7) is "Imagine," and it seems that, in the mind of this poem, as it was for the Romantics as well, imagination can be a facilitator, a bridge between conscious thought and transcendence.

I should mention that there's a lovely light music here too, mostly based on unrhymed alliterative pairings — static/pattern in lines 2–3, thorn/thicket in line 5, then whole/slowly, ash/shifts, and face/efface/presence later. It's understated, a bit of not-song in the white noise.

If the ash Buddha image seems to encourage a lingering, attentive turning away from the divine, the penultimate lines point to its inverse, an immature kind of turning away. The infant who believes that "*Not to see* is the same as *not being seen*" is clearly mistaken, and Pankey implies that those of us who turn away from the possibility of spiritual transcendence are doing the same thing. Not everyone would agree, perhaps, but I like Pankey's willingness to allow a bit of the affectionate admonishing preacher to make an appearance here.

Last point: to my mind the biggest obstacle to writing about religious experience is the massive amount of texts, histories, and arguments that have already travelled there. We probably don't wish to adhere too closely to ideas that are antiquated, but we also don't want to dismiss our predecessors just because our cellphones have better resolution. Pankey takes this challenge head on at the end of "Ash," drawing forth one more important origin text.

"God was not the fire" circles back to how the ash in Huang's *Ash Buddha* was created, but is also a reference to First Kings chapter 19, in which the prophet Elijah has a vision. It's worth quoting a bit from verses 11–12: "And behold God passed by, and a great strong wind tore into the mountains and broke the rocks in pieces, but God was not in the wind; and after the wind an earthquake, but God was not in the earthquake; and after the earthquake a fire, but God was not in the fire; and after the fire a still small voice."

Notice how much more time the biblical authors spend talking about what *isn't* God. The wind and the earthquake and the fire — such things are vividly evoked, but they are not where God can be found. Even the final phrase stops just short of pointing at God's presence. The "still small voice" is clearly intended to be seen as where "God is," but refrains from explicitly declaring it.

Why do I mention all of this? This whole poem has been circling around our struggles to connect with transcendence, to encounter God, and despite numerous near-misses we still end up where "God was not." Buddha and the God of the Hebrew Bible have made their appearances, as have Romanticism, quantum physics, and child psychology. But the God that Eric

Pankey is looking for isn't in the Buddha, but rather in the disintegrating ash. Not the bearded patriarchal God that reaches for Adam on the ceiling of the Sistine Chapel, but in the space between the fingers. Not in any vision, but in our periphery, as we turn away, pretending not to see.

"Ash" is about the *search* for God, about trying to be open to an encounter with the divine, despite its inherent, tantalizing ephemerality. What I love about this poem is that it is willing to live in its uncertainty, in fact to *articulate* that uncertainty, that longing for something just beyond our reach, freighted with conflicting traditions and frustrations, and yet still propelling us toward a higher sense of ourselves and the world.

How a Poem Mourns

Don Paterson, "Mercies"

Mercies

She might have had months left of her dog-years,
but to be who? She'd grown light as a nest
and spent the whole day under her long ears
listening to the bad radio in her breast.
On the steel bench, knowing what was taking shape
she tried and tried to stand, as if to sign
that she was still of use, and should escape
our selection. So I turned her face to mine,
and seeing only love there — which, for all

the wolf in her, she knew as well as we did —
she lay back down and let the needle enter.
And love was surely what her eyes conceded
as her stare grew hard, and one bright aerial
quit making its report back to the centre.

— from 40 Sonnets (Faber & Faber, 2015)

You probably don't need my help to appreciate the heart-breaking power of this little story, the pain and empathy that Paterson conveys. So let me just point out a few things about this poem that make it especially masterful.

Don Paterson's *40 Sonnets* proves, over and over again, that the sonnet is still a vibrant and moving form for poetry, well into the seventh century of its existence. Many of Paterson's are "perfect," in the sense that they follow the traditional form — rhyming iambic pentameter (with some standard variations), and a volta, or turn, that shapes its "argument." So the first thing to point out is the effortlessness with which Paterson shapes his sentences so that the rhymes and rhythms move fluidly, without calling too much attention to themselves, but also varying the meter enough so it doesn't go flat. Just look at the first few lines:

> u / u u / / u u / /
> She might have had months left of her dog-years,
> u / u / u / / u u /
> but to be who? She'd grown light as a nest
> u / u / / / u u / /
> and spent the whole day under her long ears
> / u u / u / / uu / u /
> listening to the bad radio in her breast.

Each line has its requisite five stresses, but no line is the same, and if you weren't looking for it, you might lose track of the meter altogether. No one would blame you. It's just as smooth and natural as conversation, but with that underlying pulse that lets you know it's composed and careful. Like a Mozart melody. Oh, by the way, if you mostly remember Shakespearean sonnet forms that conclude with a couplet, I'll mention that just as common (and older) is the Petrarchan sonnet, which always uses some variation of the 8-and-6 format: two quatrains (four-line stanzas) with a matching rhyme pattern, and then some variations of a six-line structure — here it's *abcbac*.

So what might be the "turn" in the poem? Does it fulfill that aspect of the sonnet form as well? For me, it revolves around the unasked question, "What does a dog understand?" The first two quatrains are coy about this: "knowing what was taking shape" is vague enough that we can dismiss what is meant by "knowing." Any dog would react uncomfortably on a veterinarian's "steel bench," because it would "know" or remember painful injections or minor surgeries that occurred there before. That crucial "as if" in line 6 admits that the pet may not fully understand the implications of what was happening to her. She's trying to stand up, to get off the bench, but the "understanding" that the speaker associates with her actions has more to do with her owner's guilt and sadness.

So then the turn, subtle and empathetic, is when the speaker insists on what the dog really does know. Notice it's the same verb: "knowing" in line 5 and then "knew" in line 10. The repetition is significant in a poem so short. But it's not the fear she knows, or "what was taking shape." What she knows, what her owner *insists* she knows, is love. The convoluted sentence structure hides it, buries it in qualifications and asides, but it's there:

So I turned her face to mine,
and seeing only love there — which, for all
the wolf in her, she knew as well as we did —
she lay back down and let the needle enter.

Despite the speaker's rationalizations about what has to be done to ease the animal's suffering, and despite his qualifications about her wildness ("for all / the wolf in her"), the powerful assertion that the speaker comes to realize in the poem, the "turn," is that his pet knows love as well as we do. And *that's* the moment the needle enters. It's just devastating.

This also connects me back to the title. Mercy is an important concept in a number of religious traditions. Central to it is the idea that mercy is bestowed upon us despite the fact that we haven't earned it, or even deserve it. On the one hand the act of euthanasia is an act of mercy, saving the speaker's pet from further pain and suffering. But the title is "Mercies," plural. The other mercy is bestowed upon the speaker by his beloved pet, who accepts her owner's decision, and mercifully makes the last memory he will have of her one of love and not anger or fear. One other religious connection to the title that I'm not sure Paterson is aware of: "God Full of Mercies," or El Malei Rachamim, is a prayer traditionally said at a Jewish graveside, intended to help escort the soul of the departed to heaven.

A few other quick points of admiration. First, the wonderful, transformative comparisons Paterson makes early on — the dog as "light as a nest," whose breathing is a "bad radio." Then, about halfway through, the terrifying use of the word "selection," which recalls some terrible episodes in human history. Not that Paterson is making a direct comparison — that would be absurd — but the word choice crystallizes his sense of guilt. He can't help but see, in his power to choose the very moment of his pet's death, uncomfortable correspondences.

And finally, that last sentence, with two terrific gestures. First, the word "concede" is a pun that means to admit something is true, but also to give up. "I concede your point," but also, "Once he captured my queen I conceded." So when Paterson writes that "love was surely what her eyes conceded," he means that the dog's eyes understood, agreed to what the speaker believes is an act of love. But as the needle enters, she also gives up her capacity to love, she concedes it.

The other choice is the idea that a "bright aerial / quit making its report back to the centre." In a literal sense an aerial is an antenna, and the idea that this individual aerial has ceased its transmissions recalls the "bad radio" at the beginning of the poem and is an apt metaphor for a life ending. But then what is the "centre" in this metaphor? Is it some religious idea all life being connected somehow, whether to God or some other spiritual source? The speaker doesn't need to be exactly sure, but whatever the "centre" is, this poem asserts that the dog's "report" is no less valuable and pure than that of any other life, human or otherwise. It's another way of equating the animal's spirit with the speaker's, which deepens his guilt and his grief.

How a Poem Confronts the Limitations of Our Empathy

Soraya Peerbaye, "Trials"

There are books published every year that concern themselves with incidents stripped from headlines, recent or historical. In some ways poets are mandated to respond to newsworthy events — poets give voice to our shock or astonishment, can see those events in unexpected ways, and can help guide or challenge our responses. But a poet has to be very careful in her use of the material: it's a fine line between bringing an important story to life and exploiting it.

When a poet devotes a whole collection to an obsessive examination of an incident like the murder of a teenager, the challenge is much greater. The subject threatens to overtake the poet's artistry, so that some collections descend into a kind of empty empathetic reportage, deriving their power from their subject rather than contributing something new in their own right. One friend of mine called this the "about-ness" of such books, that what they are "about" is all they are. The question of what the poet adds to the story is as crucial as the care taken with the story itself.

Soraya Peerbaye's book *Tell: poems for a girlhood* breaks through these concerns, making something meticulously observed and deeply empathetic. The poems revolve around the 1997 murder of fourteen-year-old Reena Virk near Victoria, British Columbia. In her own research Peerbaye got unusually close to the events — attending trials, walking the landscape where the events occurred. And as you'll see, she also never lets herself off the hook when engaging the material.

"Trials" is the opening poem in the book, and so has to open the door for us, to establish the situation, perhaps allude to some of the central concerns of the collection, and compel us to go further. But it also has to work as a poem on its own. I think it does.

Trials

Magnolias in bloom, each trial held in early spring.
Pink-white curve of petals like skinned knees.
Newspapers opened to her eighth grade photograph:
black curls, bronze smile, heirloom gold earring.

In the courtroom, articles of clothing suggested her.
Exhibits. Out of the pleather jacket her torso emerged;

out of her clog boots, her stance. She believed in this,
that her body could be enough. As a girl, I would have liked
to be like that, to have her daring. Still — hard to say,
if I'd have been her friend — her ardour, pungent, dangerous.

Even flowers are ranked, said the woman watching
the proceedings with me. *Roses are worth more*
than daisies. Lilies more than daffodils. I want
her body to stand, be its own testimony. Instead
it's the jacket, held before the witness,
      open, declarative,

while the fair-haired girl behind Plexiglas
says nothing.
              — from *Tell: poems for a girlhood* (Pedlar Press, 2015)

We enter the poem as we approach the courtroom, confront-
ing the dissonance between the beautiful spring landscape and
the concerns of the day. The comparison of the magnolia petals
to skinned knees is a quiet way of connecting us to a familiar
image of childhood that will take on darker tones later in the
collection as the damage done to Virk's body is detailed. This
image then merges into the school portrait of a girl with typical
features — "black hair, bronze smile, heirloom gold earring."

But we can't really get at Reena — her jacket and her shoes
only "suggest" her, as does the facial expression she wears in the
ubiquitous school photo. What the trial, and the whole book, is
about is the fact that Reena Virk is no longer here to develop and
declare her true self. Our speaker, witness not to the events but
to the *retelling* of the events, struggles to unlock the personality

behind the material remains of Reena's life. Her tentative conclusion is that the girl "believed in this, / that her body could be enough." What does the speaker mean? Enough for what? To be loved? To be happy?

In later sections of the book, the speaker of these poems will connect to Virk as a woman of colour, as someone who knew some, but not all, of the dangers and temptations Virk faced growing up. But here at the beginning of the collection we don't yet know why the speaker might be attending these trials, what her relationship is to this story. What we know is that she's prepared to interrogate it. On the one hand, she admits she "would have liked / to be like that, to have her daring." On the other hand, the details of clothing that speak "daring" to our speaker hardly seem so cutting-edge — the leather jacket, the boots — but they are enough to create a distance for our speaker, who admits that it's "hard to say, / if I'd been her friend."

This admission is the uncomfortable heart of this poem for me — it's a strange, awkward realization. "Will you be my friend?" is a child's question, and the implied answer here, we sense, is "probably not." Reena's "pungent, dangerous" "ardour" might have repelled the speaker of these poems. "Pungent" is a fantastic adjective here; it evokes the loud smells of teenagers, the sweat and perfume, potato chips and cigarettes. And so the adult who is observing all of this, the adult who is attending the trials and writing the poems, stands aside, remembers her own adolescence, and recognizes another barrier to her connection. The traits and circumstances that saved someone like her from *becoming* Reena Virk are likely the very same traits and circumstances that prevent her from calling Reena Virk a friend.

The observation made in the next stanza that "even flowers are ranked" is in some ways even more distasteful, and we'd like to think of it as fundamentally untrue. It's interesting to me that Peerbaye puts this opinion into the mouth of another person, rather than coming to the realization herself. Rather than dispute the assertion though, our reporter wants Virk's "body to . . . be its own testimony." Of course if Virk were able to be a witness for herself, she'd still be alive. But all we have is the jacket.

The jacket, and the accused. In the final, sharp little stanza, we are reminded that there *is* someone in the room who knew Reena Virk, who was in contact with Virk's body, who understood her "pungent ardour," and who made a decision not to be her friend. As our attention turns to the accused, we are very aware of her as a body that still exists — a body protected behind Plexiglas, a body with fair hair, a body that chooses to be silent. And so we face the frustration of more barriers to finding Reena Virk, but also a curiosity about this other young woman. Who is she? What traits and circumstances brought *her* to this courtroom?

If you read the rest of *Tell: poems for a girlhood*, you'll eventually hear the voices of the accused in the Virk case, and see more details about the crime, from the wounds Virk received to the landscape where it all occurred. But in "Trials," at the beginning of the book, we can only see that dark door opening. On its own, this poem points toward our inability to connect with either of these two silent, inaccessible girls, and the frustration and shame that come with the limitations of our empathy. The ending is designed to be unsatisfying because the situation is unsatisfying. We are left knowing that we will never cross the barriers that separate us from either of them.

How a Poem Tries to Get into It

Rowan Ricardo Phillips, "Little Song"

Little Song

Both guitars run trebly. One noodles
Over a groove. The other slushes chords.
Then they switch. It's quite an earnest affair.
They close my eyes. I close their eyes. A horn
Blares its inner air to brass. A girl shakes
Her ass. Some dude does the same. The music's
Gone moot. Who doesn't love it when the bass
Doesn't hide? When you can feel the trumpet peel
Old oil and spit from deep down the empty

Pit of a note or none or few? So don't
Give up on it yet: the scenario.
You know that it's just as tired of you
As you are of it. Still, there's much more to it
Than that. It does not not get you quite wrong.

— from *Heaven* (Farrar, Straus & Giroux, 2015)

Literally a sonnet is a "little song." The other rules we asso-
ciate with the form — the fourteen lines, the iambic pentameter
and rhyme schemes, the volta or turn of logic or emotion —
give the sonnet its traditional shape, but at its heart the sonnet
doesn't have to be so strict. We saw a textbook sonnet with Don
Paterson a few pages ago, but there are other poems that gesture
toward the form while sloughing off its rhyme and meter so that
we might not even notice unless we look at them again. In these
pages, Diane Seuss' "Free beer" has the requisite fourteen lines
and an emotional turn, as does Damian Rogers' "Ode to a Rolling
Blackout" and Richard Siken's "Dots Everywhere." Some tradi-
tionalists would say those poems don't qualify as sonnets, but I'm
not really interested in a yes-no debate on the subject. They're
either sonnets or they refer to the sonnet form. Either way, no
self-respecting poet can complete a fourteen-line lyric without
recognizing the tradition she is travelling in.

Here Phillips gives us a sort of syncopated sonnet, with
fourteen lines and a rough pentameter working throughout, but
the rhymes occur more often in the middle of the lines than at
the end — noodles/groove in lines 1–2, affair/blare/air in lines 3
and 5, brass/ass in 5 and 6, etc.). Why do this? First off, it gives
us the off-balance rhythm of other contemporary art forms.
But I also suspect it's because the performance being described

here is itself imperfect. So the poem is a flawed little song about a flawed little song. The turn the poem makes is in trying to find transcendence in spite of its flaws.

We open with some lukewarm descriptions of the musicians at some sort of concert. The guitarists, whose instruments "run trebly," "noodle," and "slush." These are not words we associate with rock-and-roll virtuosity. And the observation at the end of line 3, "It's quite an earnest affair," is laughably condescending. Further down he'll damn the bassist with faint praise (it's not hiding!), and even his more ambitious attempt to praise the trumpet falls apart at the end of that looping sentence. Sure, it would be nice if this horn player could "peel / old oil and spit from deep down the empty / pit of a note" but the sentence ends "or none or few." It's the "or none or few" that I love — our speaker is conflicted, trying to shut down his critical ear so that he can enter the moment. The way I read it, he's hoping the horn will "peel old oil," etc., but his critical ear says "none" and then his spiritual hope urges "few."

In other words, this isn't like C.K. Williams' "Love: Beginnings," when the sight of the couple embracing unexpectedly stirs the observer into a visceral reaction. But while he can't help but observe the band with something less than full enthusiasm, our speaker and his fellow celebrants have nevertheless decided to try to find a way to lose themselves in the music. "They close my eyes. I close their eyes" seems like a conscious effort to get *into* it. "A girl shakes / her ass. Some dude does the same" hardly seems like a high-powered dance floor scene, but at least they're moving.

Eventually "The music's / gone moot." Not *mute*, but moot, unimportant, tangential to the experience. The mediocrity of the musicians is irrelevant — we're here together, dancing. And while the poem goes back and forth, our host urges us in line 11 not to "give up on it yet." Notice he's not telling us not to give up on the band itself — they're probably never going to be worth mentioning, and Phillips has the decency to withhold from us any identifying description except for their specific instruments. So give up on the band. But don't give up on "it," the *scenario*, yes, there's hope there. The scene of a concert, a dance club, or a house party basement, surely we are still capable of losing ourselves in the music, of dancing in a crowd, despite how our experience and expertise might obstruct us from fully entering the experience. Can't we?

And the misstepping rhythm of that last line. Can I talk about the double negative for a minute? In grammar school we learned that we shouldn't use double negatives, because they cancel themselves out. "Rob is not not guilty" means Rob's guilty, of course. But "I'm not unimpressed" isn't really the same as "I'm impressed," is it? The double negative is qualified, cagey. So when Phillips double-doubles the double negative in the last line, we have to spend real time pulling apart the actual meaning of the sentence. "It does not not get you quite wrong" is a mind-bender, but in high school English class we'd just cross out a few of those "nots": "It does — not not — get you quite wrong," means "It does get you quite wrong." But all the grammatical wriggling here may also mean "it" sort of gets you a little bit right? The awkwardness of the connection doesn't mean that there *isn't* one.

So the poem is about not quite losing yourself totally in the music, but also about not *not* losing yourself in the music. The musicians aren't the best, and the speaker is held back by

How a Poem Chattily Wonders about Life's Purpose

Ulrikka S. Gernes, "On H.C. Andersen Boulevard During Rush Hour"

On H.C. Anderson Boulevard During Rush Hour

around five o'clock I'm a speck of stardust on a bicycle
wrapped in my life's nanosecond, my life's nanosecond,
my life's nanosecond and this poem that doesn't really
fit in anywhere either, and I have already wasted an infinitely
immeasurable fraction of the light intended for me, as I just
manage to glimpse the wing tip of a herring gull tear
a white cut into the air above Langebro, a tear in the blue

and there you are and there's my daughter, the strings, the wind
instruments, a tiny stage and a fragile ship ascending on
the waving pillar of smoke from a cigarette someone
tosses and butts right now under the heel against a flagstone
in the universe and a bleeding cut on the lip screams,
have I loved, have I loved, have I loved enough.

— from *Frayed Opus for Strings & Wind Instruments*
(Brick Books, 2015)

Ulrikka Gernes is a Danish poet whose collection, *Frayed Opus for Strings & Wind Instruments*, translated by Canadians Patrick Friesen and Per Brask, was a finalist for the Canadian Griffin Prize. As I mentioned when discussing Natalie Toledo's poem earlier, there's a way that a translation always belongs as much to the translator as it does to the poet. So call this a Gernes/Friesen/Brask collaboration.

So much of the pleasure for me comes from the poem's pacing, the wonderful way it circles from casual observation to more serious matters and back again, all the while giving us a vivid sense of the speaker's journey downtown. We get our first feel for that pacing with the threefold repetition of "my life's nanosecond." We know already (from line 2) that she is on a bicycle, and the repetition feels like the turning of the wheels. But that particular phrase — "my life's nanosecond" — lets us know a bit more about the speed at which she's travelling: not as quick as it would be if it were "my life my life my life," for example. Also, the lines are on the long side, which makes them read a bit like prose, at a fairly brisk pace, but the frequent enjambments incrementally slow us down, like a stop sign along the way. Our speaker's journey seems purposeful but not harried. It's a pace that allows her mind to wander a bit.

H.C. Andersen Boulevard, by the way, is one of the main thoroughfares in downtown Copenhagen, where Gernes lives. The street is named, of course, for the writer Hans Christian Andersen, whom most of us know from his versions of fairy tales like "The Princess and the Pea," "The Little Mermaid," and "The Emperor's New Clothes." It's worth noting that many of his tales, while ostensibly for children, have plenty of implications for adults as well.

But I don't want to burden the poem by reading too much symbolism into the names of streets. Whatever quiet sense we have of the significance of Andersen's stories on the way we encounter the poem, H.C. Andersen Boulevard is also a perfectly normal way for a mother to make her way from work or home to meet a daughter and friend. (By the way, the Langebro is a bridge that leads to the Boulevard.) The sense we have of the speaker's active, wandering mind as she travels is the central characteristic of the poem.

And where does her mind go? Only to some of the most important questions about how we spend our lives: "I have already wasted an infinitely / immeasurable fraction of the light intended for me" is terrific. First, because the "infinitely immeasurable" is both scientifically accurate and a little ridiculous. Second, because of the inspired way Gernes measures life: in light. The comparison I can't help but make is to T.S. Eliot's famous line "I have measured out my life with coffee spoons." How much more wonderful and precious is a life that is measured in light?

So we have at once a whimsical and deeply serious self-questioning about how the speaker has made use of her time on Earth. For me this combination is rare good company. Then a quick image of a common seabird and we're ready to learn the purpose of the journey — to meet "you" and "my daughter." I'm not 100 percent sure, but it seems that there's a concert — perhaps a school performance? There are strings and wind instruments, as well as a "tiny stage." Are these literal or metaphoric? And the "fragile ship ascending on / the waving pillar of smoke from a cigarette" could be an affectionate description of music played by students, or it could be an image of a vessel on the waterways the speaker has just traversed. In these lines I'm less sure of what we're doing than I am of why we're doing it.

A quick point about the relationships here: the daughter is not "ours," she's "my daughter." In other words, she does not also belong to "you." So we can presume that "you" is either a friend or a new romantic relationship. Whatever the connection, the fact that "you" is there demonstrates a certain level of commitment too, especially if the meeting is for a school performance. Most of us, I'd venture to say, don't voluntarily attend the school performances of other people's children.

In other words, these lines begin to answer the question posed by the final line of the poem. The repeated "have I loved, have I loved, have I loved enough" is a kind of counterpoint to the repeated phrases about "life's nanosecond." But instead of worrying about how much time she's *wasted*, now we're more focused on how well she's used what light she *has*.

The truth is that the answer to the question "Have I loved enough" is always "No." We can always love more; it's not a finite resource. Asking the question of ourselves is a way for the speaker to focus her attention, to urge herself to strive for more.

And I suspect that, by riding her bicycle to meet her daughter and friend for a concert or whatever, the speaker of this poem has begun to try to respond to the challenge. Which is why she closes the curtain on us now — the rest of the afternoon is not for whimsical literary observations or life evaluation. It's for her daughter and her friend.

How a Poem Transforms a Stroll into a Ceremony

Joy Harjo, "Walk"

Walk

Dead umbrella — broken wings
Carryout Styrofoam — chicken grease
Crow rain — orange peel in beak.
Blue wad of gum — one day I will sleep.
Ferns drinking rain — I am thirsty for sun.
Winds from up north — lounge here in this mist.
Black squirrel on a slag of stone — carry me home.

Giant tree roots are highway of ant trade routes — where do I
    belong?
Crisp holly with red berries — we are holy with hope.
Another dead umbrella — we are getting wet.
Winds' cousins — fly up behind them.
Clouds slip to earth —
All this walking and I'm not getting far.
Water spirit feeling . . . round my head —
Where will I go when I am dead?

Vancouver, BC

— from *Conflict Resolution for Holy Beings*
(W.W. Norton & Company, 2015)

One of the reasons Joy Harjo's *Conflict Resolution for Holy Beings* was selected for the Griffin Prize shortlist was the range of things she can do with a poem. There are blues lyrics and Mvskoke rituals, poems about Hawaii and DFW Airport, brief prose interludes and sprawling narratives. She can be matter-of-fact about ancient rituals and ecstatic about jazz saxophone, or she can combine them all into one multi-faceted poem to make something uniquely her own. In "Walk," we get a quick glimpse of Harjo's ability to switch tones, with a hint of the wit she uses to inject the spiritual into the mundane and vice versa.

The situation of the poem seems pretty straightforward — the speaker is going for a walk, and is recording images she encounters and thoughts she has along the way. As with Ulrikka Gernes' poem, there's a liberating sense in a poem like this that the speaker might take us anywhere. A walker can be drawn to her landscape, but does not have to be constrained by it; she can draw a range of connections. Harjo is not as chatty as Gernes, and moves at a slower pace (Gernes is on a bicycle . . .), but there's a similar sweep that's available to her.

Structurally "Walk" uses a loose two-part form in each line, with em-dashes in between, a kind of pairing that reminds me of Old English alliterative verse, or even biblical parallelism. All of these forms set two lines or phrases up against each other, and then explore different ways of connecting them. For example, the first pairing, "Dead umbrella — broken wings," is a metaphoric comparison: umbrella $\cong$ wings. The second, "Carryout Styrofoam — chicken grease," feels like a way of looking more closely at some garbage on the street, adding specific detail. Oh, it's chicken grease as opposed to bacon grease or maple syrup.

To me these opening lines are a rhythmic set-up, the way a jazz tune will start with two repetitions of a melody in order to establish its chord progression. Once it's clear in the listener's mind, the soloists can range freely, knowing that we can still hear the original structure underneath. By starting these pairings with simpler structures — metaphor, elaboration — Harjo prepares us to go further afield.

By the way, the technical term for the pause in the middle of the line is caesura, which acts as a pause, but also like half of a line break. Here it also makes me think of steps as Harjo's speaker continues her walk.

As we move along, things start to get a bit more complicated. What is "Crow rain"? Is it a specific kind of rain (as opposed to "goose rain" or "squirrel rain")? Or is the speaker using a bit of shorthand to describe what she sees — crow, rain. The "orange peel in beak" seems to suggest the latter, but if it's the first I have a fun time wondering what the metaphoric "orange peel" might be in a crow rain — a ray of sunshine, perhaps? As a reader I feel the possibilities expanding.

Our speaker's personal concerns enter the scene in line 4: "Blue wad of gum — one day I will sleep." I find this hilarious — the speaker sees some discarded, flavourless gum on the street and somehow connects it to her exhaustion. Does she also feel chewed up and spit out? It could be a moody response to a depressing bit of litter, but the image seems witty to me, as if she's daring us to make that overwrought comparison. Before it strikes us as maudlin she moves on.

In line 5, "Ferns drinking rain" seems to summon a "but" before its accompanying "I am thirsty for sun." And in the lines that follow we begin to construct the mood in which our friend is taking this walk — the weather is gloomy, she's tired and missing her sunnier landscapes. There's also a creeping question about her place in the world — "carry me home" in line 7 (addressed to the squirrel?) is followed almost immediately by "where do I belong?" Meanwhile though, she can't help but turn her sharp eye to the world around her — the north winds that "lounge here in this mist," the "slag of stone," the "ant trade routes." These imagistic flourishes keep reminding us that these musings, these questions, are happening in a physical landscape, a real part of the world where the squirrels are black and the wind lounges in the mist.

The highlight of the poem for me is this couplet:

Crisp holly with red berries — we are holy with hope.
Another dead umbrella — we are getting wet.

The delight is following the speaker's back and forth between the profound and the self-deprecatingly practical. "Holy with hope" feels like a discovery, the kind of blip of inspiration that inspires poets to go for long walks in the rain. But the next line reminds us of the body, the soaking wet, grumpy body. Again I hear Harjo's wit at work here, undercutting the alliterative, soaring ambition of "we are holy with hope" with the blunt, balloon-popping, "Another broken umbrella — we are getting wet." Just as every outdoor image now has its internal counterpart, so too does each stretch toward the spiritual have its counterpart in the mundane, dripping world.

Harjo ends with the longest two pairings, and reverses the pattern of following her more abstract questions with an awareness of the physical world. Here the frustration of "all this walking and I'm not getting far" transforms into something resembling prayer:

> Clouds slip to earth —
> All this walking and I'm not getting far.
> *Water spirit feeling . . . round my head* —
> Where will I go when I am dead?

We also have our first italics. To me it sounds as if the "water spirit feeling" that the speaker feels hovering "round my head" is now the addressee of the final question, as if these musings and observations have a divine audience. The speaker's initial response to a rainy Vancouver day — when it feels like water is absolutely everywhere — now is something more, something profound and unique, a "water spirit feeling." And once she feels that spirit near, her question is one of humanity's oldest: "Where will I go when I am dead?" After Harjo has done so much to ground her larger concerns in the mundane world, this ending feels less like a doctrinaire inquiry into the heavenly afterlife, and more a curiosity about the cycles of earthly life — water or earth, holly or wind? Or perhaps it's a request for directions: Hey water spirit, when I'm dead, where will I go — any recommendations? For me these closing lines bring together Harjo's matter-of-fact spirituality, her magical vision of the natural world around her, and her profound humour, all in a deceptively simple-sounding package.

How a Poem Imperfectly Reconciles Complexity

Liz Howard, "A Wake"

A Wake

Your eyes open the night's slow static at a loss
to explain this place you've returned to from above;
cedar along a broken shore, twisting in a wake of fog.

I've lived in rooms with others, of no place and no mind
trying to bind a self inside the contagion of words while
your eyes open the night's slow static. At a loss

to understand all that I cannot say, as if you came
upon the infinite simply by thinking and it was
a shore of broken cedar twisting in a wake of fog.

If I moan from an animal throat it is in hope you
will return to me what I lost learning to speak.
Your eyes open the night's slow static at a loss

to ever know the true terminus of doubt, the limits of skin.
As long as you hold me I am doubled from without and within:
a wake of fog unbroken, a shore of twisted cedar.

I will press myself into potential, into your breath,
and maybe what was lost will return in sleep once I see
your eyes open into the night's slow static, at a loss.
Broken on a shore of cedar. We twist in a wake of fog.

— from *Infinite Citizen of the Shaking Tent*
(McClelland & Stewart, 2015)

Liz Howard's *Infinite Citizen of the Shaking Tent* won the Canadian Griffin Prize for Poetry the year that I was a juror. One thing in particular that compels me about the collection is how ambitiously it tries to work through a bunch of different conflicts and identities. Howard is part indigenous, part settler; she's part neuroscientist and part poet; she's from northern Ontario but lives in urban Toronto. In her poems, she's often exploring the turmoil of these competing influences and trying to find a path that, if it doesn't exactly reconcile them, at least captures the tension between them.

I hope by now it goes without saying: poems often don't have full answers to the problems they present. They are not essays or sermons or treatises. It's enough (for me, at least) that Howard's poems provide us with a rich glimpse into a complex, fraught, very modern situation.

This can make for some dense reading. So I'm going to take a little extra time with this one, hoping you'll be patient with me. In the first lines the "you," whomever the speaker is addressing, seems to be having a bit of trouble re-acclimating themselves to "this place you've returned to from above." That "from above" is interesting — on the one hand, it could be a simple reference to a plane ride. On the other, there might be an implication that the speaker has somehow "moved up" in the world, and that this visit is somehow a return to a "lower self." More on that "lower self" in a minute. We're also going to have to think more about who this "you" is.

Meanwhile, you can hear Howard's rich acoustic music with staticky sounds peppering that first line: "the night'S Slow Static at a loSS." There's something thick, fraught, and even laboured in the way the poem opens. There's just no way you can say "night's slow static" as quickly as you can say, for example, "evening's leisurely confusions," despite the fact that the second option means roughly the same thing and has twice as many syllables. So we have a deliberate pace, and a figure who is having trouble explaining a new life to an older, familiar one.

In the next stanza, the speaker notes that while her companion has been living this new life, she herself has lived in different places "trying to bind myself inside a contagion of words." What does she mean by this? Is the poem itself a "contagion of words"?

If so, why would she deliberately try to bind herself inside it? Is language a kind of prison, or an infection?

If we aren't yet sure, it seems that the speaker's companion shares our confusion. He is "At a loss // to understand all I cannot say." (I'm using "he" just to keep things clear for now — there's no real indication of the companion's gender. In fact there isn't really a clear subject at all for this sentence, so it may be the "I" who is at a loss. More on this shortly.) Our speaker seems to admire her friend because of something instinctual in his own approach to spiritual matters: you "came upon the infinite simply by thinking," something she cannot do.

By now you might have noticed something about the last lines of each stanza. They're not exactly the same, but they're close, alternating between being "at a loss," with some accompanying "static," and a line about "twisting in a wake of fog." So now we have to talk about the form of the poem, which is a rough villanelle.

You may have studied villanelles in school. There are some famous villanelles (Dylan Thomas' "do not go gentle into that good night," or Elizabeth Bishop's "One Art" are both terrific) that reward a close reading. The technical definition is that a strict villanelle repeats line 1 and 3 verbatim at the end of alternating stanzas, and then together in the final four-line stanza. Those two repeating lines should also rhyme. And the middle lines of each stanza are also supposed to rhyme with each other. If that sounds difficult, let me provide you a nonsense example so you can see how it all fits together:

> Blahdy blahdy blahdy blahdy blah.
> So yo so yo so yo so yo so yo,
> Wadi wadi wadi wadi wah.

Toddy toddy toddy toddy tah,
Froyo froyo froyo froyo fro.
Blahdy blahdy blahdy blahdy blah.

Hottie hottie hottie hottie hah!
This is kind of tricky, don't you know?
Wadi wadi wadi wadi wah.

(a couple more stanzas varying the two above and then:)

Hahvahd's where I pahked my wicked cah
I hope I'll soon let all this madness go.
Blahdy blahdy blahdy blahdy blah.
Wadi wadi wadi wadi wah.

"A Wake" is not a strict villanelle (the first lines in each stanza don't rhyme, the meter is irregular), but it follows the pattern of repeating the final phrases of those two alternating lines — the cedar broken and twisting in a wake of fog in the first repeated line, and then "Your eyes open the night's slow static at a loss," which is repeated more consistently. Villanelles lend themselves to a kind of unsolvable argument — Bishop's "art of losing is hard to master" set against "disaster," or Thomas' "do not go gentle into that good night" vs. "rage, rage." With the two lines juxtaposed against each other at the ending, villanelles tend to suspend their points of contention rather than resolve them.

Okay, so now we might be able to see where this is headed, with the companion figure and the speaker representing contrasting approaches to life that may not find full reconciliation by the end. Meanwhile though, we're going to reacquaint ourselves with the body in the fourth stanza. "If I moan from an animal throat it is in hope you / will return to me what I lost learning to speak." I read the speaker's "animal throat" as a possible reference to the sexual pleasures that return us to our most basic animal selves. If the visiting friend is indeed a lover, it's as if their passion will help our speaker release some of her concerns about being trapped in language.

I should mention that this idea of being trapped in language, or falling into it, is likely a reference to the psychological theories of Jacques Lacan. There's not *remotely* enough space here to offer a full explanation of Lacan's ideas about language, but for someone like Howard, who is trained in literary studies *and* neuroscience, Lacan is a difficult figure to escape. Lacan suggests that language directs the way we make meaning — not only of the outside world, but also of ourselves. The speaker seems to be aware that if that's true, then her study of Lacan and other psychologists must also change the way she *is*. She's caught in a kind of infinite loop: in striving to understand her identity (and perhaps advance her education and her professional prospects) she is also changing her identity, so she can't quite make sense of herself.

Heady stuff. So no wonder that "moan[ing] from an animal throat" is a longed-for act of counterbalance. The "self I lost learning to speak," in its most basic form, returns our speaker to a more innocent self, whether that self is a childhood self, a prehistoric self, or at least a self before literary theory. The lines that follow suggest that love might quiet the noise, the static, that is clouding the speaker's identity. In this reading, a line like "As long as you hold me I am doubled from without and within," makes her multiplication an expansion, a doubling she can embrace. Another line that expresses hope in the redemptive power of romantic love is: "I will press myself into potential, into your breath," and then, "maybe what was lost will return in sleep once I see your eyes open." In this reading of the poem, there's hope for a way of living that includes love *and* language, growth and remembering, the theoretical mind and the twisting body.

But there's another reading too. I assigned this book to a class, and one of my students convincingly read the poem as a conversation between the speaker and her other identity (shout out to Laura Ashwood from VIC165!). This may make the moaning and the "as long as you hold me" less erotic, but if the speaker is torn between two aspects of her*self*, then the "union" she makes is even more of a coming-of-age proposition. "I will press myself into potential" connects richly with the "above" we were wondering about in the first stanza, and the "you" who visits her past and embraces her roots is the same "you" who awakens and tries to reconcile her conflicted identities. As long as the "you" in the mirror holds "me" then her growth and possibilities are infinite.

It's worth noting as I close that "A Wake" is a wonderful tri-part pun that can refer to the disturbances a boat or plane leaves behind, to a memorial ceremony for a lost loved one, and as one word ("awake") as an expression of emerging consciousness, one that is ready to set about an active life. The poem embodies lots of internal conflict but also turns it into a kind of love song, a love song to a conflicted person's variousness. I'm not sure she wants to reconcile all of these parts, but if they can "twist in a wake of fog," then they are active, moving, struggling, alive.

How a Poem Haunts

Norman Dubie, "Lines for Little Mila"

Norman Dubie's poems are like no one else's I've read. The leaps of logic he makes, the moral ambition, and the allusive sweep can be dizzying. Of course that makes it hard to write short essays about most of the poems in *The Quotations of Bone*, which won the International Griffin Prize in 2016. Most of the poems are also longer than the ones I've covered here. But there are a few shorter poems that give a sense of what he's capable of. As usual, I hope a walk through this one will encourage you to dive deeper into Dubie's work.

Lines for Little Mila

Here, in a cloud of rising flour
she dabs at her chin — aging
leaves a blemish just like this . . .
the egg behind the cloud
of flour now falling
to a black mica counter.

Grandmother with a coffee tin
full of raw milk. The sun
gone beyond the mountains
long before it's gone from us.

Men cleaning fish, husking
corn on the porch.

I told a friend's little girl
about some of this,
and she immediately
slumbered, putting
a blue ghost inside my chest.

I said to her —
so you still remember things from the other side?
Then quickly I added —

of that river?
                    — from *The Quotations of Bone* (Copper Canyon Press, 2015)

We begin with a girl making a mess of the kitchen — a cloud of flour, an egg dropped on the counter. It's a domestic scene that's observed so carefully, so patiently, that it's clear no one is too concerned about the cleanup. There's a hint that there are larger concerns afoot though: a spot of flour on the girl's chin reminds our speaker that "aging / leaves a blemish just like this . . . " For me, it's the ellipsis that makes this aside resonate. An ellipsis points to something missing, somewhere the speaker is unwilling to go, a train of thought that he refuses to complete. The implication then would be about other blemishes that age leaves on us? Is *noticing* the kinds of blemishes aging bestows on us one of the blemishes aging bestows on us? So that even a pleasant evening with friends has about it some considerations of time passing, of mortality?

Musically this first stanza is just sheer pleasure — please do yourself a favour and read it out loud. It's not about internal rhyme, the way we've seen elsewhere, but about the tight lusciousness of phrases like "black mica counter," or even the deceptively matter-of-fact "leaves a blemish just like this," with its repeated *l*'s, *s*'s, and *i*'s.

In the second stanza, Grandma appears "with a coffee tin / full of raw milk." If the milk is "raw" and carried in a tin, the implication is it was probably drawn fresh from the animal, so now we know we are in the country, perhaps on a farm. But we hear no scolding from Grandma; rather we are made aware of the lingering evening, "The sun / gone beyond the mountains / long before it's gone from us." We are fortunate here; we get the sun longer than elsewhere.

So we have at first a feeling of plenty, of leisure, with multiple people around, plenty of food, and a spirit of friendship.

Our speaker is alive to all of these sensual pleasures, especially because he doesn't seem responsible for any of the preparations. Everyone else is putting the meal together — baking something with flour, cleaning fish, husking corn — but our speaker is at liberty to tell stories to Mila, inducing her to sleep. Perhaps that *is* his job — as anyone with a family knows, amusing or a-snoozing a small child can be an essential part of meal preparation. In all, despite our awareness of the passage of time, the mood is still light.

Things turn a bit in the poem when the sleeping girl puts "a blue ghost inside my chest." What exactly is a blue ghost? Now, I've read enough Norman Dubie to wonder if this is a specific allusion, but I admit I don't really know what it is. I know of a children's book called *The Blue Ghost*, as well as a tunnel in Ontario known as the Blue Ghost, and there are the Pac-Man ghosts that you can eat when you turn them blue. But I don't think those are it.

Let me say one thing about this problem, about allusion. Many readers I know worry that they are "missing something" when they read poems, particularly poems that seem to be consciously referring to other poems or works of art. It can feel like you're watching the thirteenth episode of a television show without having seen the first twelve — except the series has been on the air for 3000 years. And while you might be able to find a *Game of Thrones* wiki to help you locate a forgotten character from season 4, poems (especially recent poems) don't always provide us with the roadmap to catch every reference. But we can't get too hung up on catching *all* the allusions, or we risk missing the trees for what the forest refers to. Allusions can add to the pleasure of reading a poem, pointing to a source that can comment on, or enrich a scene or situation. Most poets will plant a signpost if we *need* the source in order to understand. Dubie himself includes a lot of his allusions right in his titles — "Winter's Grosse Fuge," "Homage to Sesshu (1420–1506)," etc. — so we can do our bit of homework before we read the poem. If not, we have to proceed knowing we might miss a brilliant little detail in the painting, but that we can appreciate the larger vision nevertheless.

So are we missing something here? Maybe. But we can also fall back on the physical sensation of the blue ghost as the speaker experiences it. What does it feel like to have a "blue ghost in my chest"? The image is strange and evocative of melancholy, an awareness of death, but also a kind of beauty. Anyone who has had a child fall asleep while telling her a story knows how exquisite that pleasure is. The fact that this speaker calls that pleasure a "blue ghost" tells me a lot about *his* state of mind. With the "blemish" of aging from the first stanza still fresh in my ear, it's not too far a leap to see that our concerns, even in this ideal scene, are increasingly focused on mortality, but with a bittersweetness that's haunting more than it is terrifying.

With an awareness of the fleeting nature of life's pleasures, our speaker can't help but be reminded of the legend, common to many traditions, that the very young have some memory of the world beyond from which they come. And so he asks the child — who is asleep, and who probably could not answer anyhow — *"so you still remember things from the other side?"* It's a surprising moment of vulnerability and exposure from a speaker who has, until this point, kept a dignified composure. His yearning to know what's out beyond our life is suddenly bare, and almost childish in its simplicity. "Do you know what it's like?"

But right away he recovers himself, nearly, "quickly" adding *of that river?* Even to himself, then, he tucks his more profound question into a more mundane one, possibly about the child's wanderings earlier in the day. Of course, we who have overheard him are not fooled. Nor is he, really. It's just the casual cover-up he uses so that he can enjoy the rest of the evening. Or the type of lie-to-move-on that we usually associate with children. But when it comes to facing death, we are all children.

What I love about this poem is how it manages to move effortlessly through some very serious material — our fascination with childhood, our profound terrifying ignorance in the face of death, our human need to put those fears away in order to enjoy life's pleasures, our inability to completely divest ourselves of the legends that we have inherited, and our quaint efforts to mask those feelings under an older person's language. That's a lot of ground to cover in twenty-one lines, especially in the midst of this busy dinner party, but I still leave this poem, like its speaker, feeling haunted.

CONCLUSION:
A FEW HOPES

So? Did you see the goldfinch?

Early on I started seeing this project as a sort of field guide. What is a field guide supposed to do? It's designed to accompany us on our travels, to give us tools to see better, to make connections, to listen. But at its core all a field guide really wants to do is transmit enthusiasm: Love the Birds of Ontario as much as I do! So, even if you haven't been magically transformed into expert ornithologists, I hope I did transmit some of my enthusiasm for poetry itself, and how it moves.

When I was rereading the manuscript for this book, editing out typos and cleaning up some excess verbiage, I noticed how often I use the word "delight" in these pages. I associate that particular word with the pleasure I get watching someone do something really well. Hearing a guitar virtuoso, seeing an actress at the height of her powers, cheering a spectacular penalty kick goal, or even witnessing a four-year-old child charm his mother into a trip to the ice cream truck. There are also forms of delight that take training to appreciate: anyone can admire a high-flying dunk, but only those who know basketball a bit better can appreciate the screen that set free the dunker. So if this book has accomplished anything, I hope it's given you a chance to see the screen.

At the end of the day, all art must begin with pleasure, even if it also wants to teach us important things about life. That doesn't mean that our taste for pleasure has to be narrow or simple. I mean "pleasure" in the broadest possible sense, and I hope these essays have helped you along a path toward finding pleasure, or even delight, in poems that are complex, mysterious, silly, dark, or all of the above. Poems are sometimes difficult not just to irritate us, but because they have complicated ideas to explore, or because they aren't sure themselves how to feel or see the world. We can also find delight in poems that tell stories, that use traditional forms, that remind us what poetry has always done with skill and passion.

Please remember that I'm just one teacher, and there are plenty of people who could teach the thirty-five poems contained here in very different ways. I'm confident that you yourself saw things that I missed or neglected in my readings. And there are hundreds, *thousands* of terrific poems that could have been included alongside or instead of those I've chosen. Those discrepancies between readers are not a mistake on your part or mine — on the contrary. They are what makes art a rich and essential human activity. There isn't only one correct answer. We respond differently, we see things from different angles and perspectives, and we catch different references. That's part of the fun. So challenge my readings, disagree with your neighbour, start a debate. The poems can handle it.

But what I really hope you *won't* do, if you've managed to finish this book, or even if you've skimmed it, is walk around the world thinking you "don't get poetry." If you still believe that, after getting this far, then this book has failed. It's my personal mission to ban the phrase "don't get poetry" from modern usage. It is an insult to your abilities as a reader, and to poetry itself.

So whether this is the first or the four-hundredth book you've read that has poems in it, I very much hope it won't be the last. The best and the worst thing about learning to love an art form is that the more we learn about it, the more we want to learn. So if I've managed to light a fire in you that puts a drain on your resources, I'm sorry not sorry. I firmly believe that poetry deserves a portion of your time, disposable income, and attention, and that it will repay your investments at a very high rate of return. There's a whole world of great poems out there to explore. It's been my great honour to be your guide for a few hours. I wish you much delight in your future travels.

Notes on Permissions

I'd like to thank all of the poets and publishers who have granted their kind permission to use the poems included here.

Madhur Anand, "Especially in a Time," from *New Index for Predicting Catastrophes* (McClelland & Stewart, 2015).

Oliver Bendorf, "Queer Facts about Vegetables," from *The Spectral Wilderness* (The Kent State University Press, 2015).

Ali Blythe, "Shattered," from *Twoism* (Goose Lane Editions, 2015).

Deborah Digges, "Stealing Lilacs in the Cemetery," from *Vesper Sparrows* (Atheneum, 1986).

Norman Dubie, "Lines for Little Mila," from *The Quotations of Bone* (Copper Canyon Press, 2015).

Marilyn Dumont, "How to Make Pemmican," from *The Pemmican Eaters* (ECW Press, 2015).

Raoul Fernandes, "Life with Tigers," from *Transmitter and Receiver* (Nightwood Editions, 2015).

"Ode to Drinking Water from My Hands" from *Catalog of Unabashed Gratitude,* by Ross Gay, 2015. Reprinted by permission of the University of Pittsburgh Press.

"On H.C. Andersen Boulevard During Rush Hour" from *Frayed Opus for Strings & Wood Instruments* by Ulrikka S. Gernes, translated from the Danish by Per Brask and Patrick Friesen (Brick Books, 2015).

Joy Harjo, "Walk," from *Conflict Resolution for Holy Beings* (Norton, 2015).

Sarah Holland-Batt, "Botany," from *The Hazards* (University of Queensland Press, 2015).

Liz Howard, "A Wake," from *Infinite Citizen of the Shaking Tent* (McClelland & Stewart, 2015).

Richard Siken, "Dots Everywhere," from *War of the Foxes* (Copper Canyon Press, 2015).

Bren Simmers, "[Night of nesting dolls]," from *Hastings-Sunrise* (Nightwood Editions, 2015).

Donna Stonecipher, "Model City [4]," from *Model City* (Shearsman Books, 2015).

Natalia Toledo, "Flower That Drops Its Petals," from *The Black Flower and Other Zapotec Poems,* translated by Clare Sullivan (Phoneme Media, 2015).

"Love: Beginnings" from *Collected Poems* by C.K. Williams. Copyright © 2006 by C.K. Williams. Reprinted by permission of Farrar, Straus and Giroux.

Tiphanie Yanique, "My brother comes to me," from *Wife* (Peepal Tree Press, 2015).

Acknowledgements

A few thank-yous: first, to the Griffin Poetry Foundation, its trustees, and to my fellow jurors Tracy K. Smith and Alice Oswald, for making my experience as a juror such a fulfilling one. Second, to the 630 or so poets and their publishers who submitted to the prize in 2015, providing me with such good company. There are people in the world who worry about poetry's excesses, its profusion, its difficulty, or its neglect, but I have no doubt we are living in a golden age for the art form. Its range, depth, virtuosity, and diversity make it a good thing on this Earth that has room for everyone. Some proof, I hope, is in these pages.

Thanks also to the individual poets whose poems I've written about here, who responded to my project with such enthusiasm and support, and to their publishers, who made the securing of permissions relatively painless.

Thanks to some early readers, who encouraged and challenged me, and who helped spread the word: Jonathan Bennett, Tzippy Cohen, Jacob McArthur Mooney, George Murray, Lisa Richler, Martha Sharpe, Michelle Shulman, Paul Vermeersch, and Roberta Sol. Yeah, that last one is my mom, and in many ways she is my ideal reader for these essays: intelligent, curious, open-minded, impatient with pretention, a little intimidated by poetry, but willing to open herself up to the chance of being moved. Whatever skills I have developed as a teacher begin with my first.

Thanks to everyone at ECW and especially Michael Holmes, who saw a book here before I did. And to Emily Schultz for copy-editing all of my ridiculous old-man spacing mistakes.

And lastly thanks to Yael and our boys, for indulging my enthusiasms.

Adam Sol is an award-winning poet, writer, and teacher. He has published four collections of poetry, including *Crowd of Sounds*, which won Ontario's Trillium Book Award. He lives in Toronto, Ontario, with his wife, Rabbi Yael Splansky, and their three sons.